NEW DIRECTIONS FOR ADULT AND CONTINUING EDUCATION

Susan Imel, *Ohio State University*
EDITOR-IN-CHIEF

D0981061

Accelerated Learning for Adults

The Promise and Practice of Intensive Educational Formats

Raymond J. Wlodkowski
Regis University, Denver

Carol E. Kasworm
North Carolina State University

EDITORS

Number 97, Spring 2003

JOSSEY-BASS
San Francisco

ACCELERATED LEARNING FOR ADULTS: THE PROMISE AND PRACTICE OF INTENSIVE EDUCATIONAL FORMATS
Raymond J. Wlodkowski, Carol E. Kasworm (eds.)
New Directions for Adult and Continuing Education, no. 97
Susan Imel, Editor-in-Chief

Microfilm copies of issues and articles are available in 16mm and 35mm, as well as microfiche in 105mm, through University Microfilms Inc., 300 North Zeeb Road, Ann Arbor, Michigan 48106-1346.

ISSN 1052-2891   electronic ISSN 1536-0717

NEW DIRECTIONS FOR ADULT AND CONTINUING EDUCATION is part of The Jossey-Bass Higher and Adult Education Series and is published quarterly by Wiley Subscription Services, Inc., a Wiley company, at Jossey-Bass, 989 Market Street, San Francisco, California 94103-1741. Periodicals postage paid at San Francisco, California, and at additional mailing offices. Postmaster: Send address changes to New Directions for Adult and Continuing Education, Jossey-Bass, 989 Market Street, San Francisco, California, 94103-1741.

SUBSCRIPTIONS cost $70.00 for individuals and $149.00 for institutions, agencies, and libraries.

EDITORIAL CORRESPONDENCE should be sent to the Editor-in-Chief, Susan Imel, ERIC/ACVE, 1900 Kenny Road, Columbus, Ohio 43210-1090. e-mail: imel.1@osu.edu.

Cover photograph by Wernher Krutein/PHOTOVAULT © 1990.

www.josseybass.com

CONTENTS

EDITORS' NOTES

A few years ago, Peter Drucker rather pessimistically predicted, "Thirty years from now . . . universities won't survive. It's as large a change as when we first got the printed book. . . .The greatest educational needs of tomorrow are . . . on the learning side" (Lenzer and Johnson, 1997, p. 127). Although the leaders of higher education may not have fully agreed with him (buildings named for the donor are still the sexiest items in a university's capital campaign), adult educators, by virtue of professional experience, are keenly aware of the growing needs of nontraditional learners for access to and efficiency of learning. They see the importance of serving older adult students with relevant, quality learning experiences that result in better workforce skills and pragmatic proficiencies. They seek out innovative possibilities for serving adults through alternative learning formats, creative schedules, and on-line delivery systems. In recent years, a frontrunner among these major innovative efforts has been accelerated learning. As noted in this volume, the Center for the Study of Accelerated Learning has identified 250 U.S. colleges and universities that offer accelerated degree programs. In addition, accelerated degree programs are found in England, Puerto Rico, the Philippines, and Australia.

Created to meet the learning needs of working adults within the time constraints of their lives and responsibilities, accelerated learning programs have strong advocates and strong critics. The advocates believe that adults, fueled by their capabilities and motivation, can accomplish quality learning through a variety of formats. Because these programs are crafted with time-intensive learning experiences, they serve well adults who want to prosper in a society where the national norms are individualism, abundance, and merit. In the eyes of these educators, it seems reasonable that adults who can commit to time-shortened schedules and have a rich background of work experiences might even excel in accelerated learning programs. They regard adults who are actively engaged in the learning worlds of work, family, and community as possessing the complex cognitive schemas to learn quickly and comprehensively. Supported by these beliefs, most accelerated learning programs typically focus on active learning strategies that engage adults in the application of new learning in realistic experiences beyond the classroom. In fact, adjunct faculty, the primary instructors in most accelerated programs, are publicly touted by their institutions for their currency and relevance to the world of work.

Critics, however, question whether quality learning can occur in time-intensive formats because the faculty must compress the curriculum and the breadth of coverage. Metaphorically, learning under such conditions becomes a shrub rather than a tree. The critics mistrust accelerated programs because students must learn a significant amount of information quickly in a shortened time period, while at the same time maintaining a full-time job and often meeting the demands of family and community involvement. They also question a system where the commercialization of learning is transparently evident, where degrees are advertised as "quickly reached goals," and a faster turnover of students can mean greater profits.

This volume offers the first major written examination of the growing world of accelerated learning in adult higher education. It conveys what accelerated learning is as it is practiced in most colleges and universities. Readers can find out how intensive learning formats are structured, developed, and assessed. This volume offers theories and research to explain why accelerated programs are flourishing and are serving as magnets for adult participation and learning. This volume will not end the debate about accelerated learning, but it does provide evidence that accounts for how accelerated learning programs will continue to gain in popularity as well as transform the face of modern higher education.

Most of the chapter authors have had extensive experience with intensive learning programs. As teachers, administrators, and researchers, they have toiled to sustain this innovation. That work, to some extent, biases their writing in favor of accelerated learning programs. However, the authenticity on which their reflections are based is, in our opinion, knowledge worth considering in higher education.

Raymond J. Wlodkowski begins the volume with an overview of the landscape of accelerated learning as a program and educational format for adults. Offering a discussion about the controversy as well as the evidence for quality in accelerated learning programs, this chapter defines the place of these programs in contemporary higher education and their attraction for adult learners. The author presents informative research regarding student performance, persistence, and success in accelerated learning programs.

The next two chapters focus on key research to amplify the salient characteristics and concepts that explain the success of accelerated learning courses and programs. In Chapter Two, Carol E. Kasworm presents a case study of adult learners' experiences in an accelerated degree program. She explores their perceptions as they proceed through a cohort-based approach to accelerated learning. Based on her analysis, she offers a conceptual model of the initial attractors and motivators for adult involvement in accelerated learning formats. Patricia A. Scott in Chapter Three provides a comprehensive overview of research regarding how students experience time-intensive courses and what factors contribute to high-quality intensive courses.

The next three chapters examine current best practices in accelerated learning programs. In Chapter Four, Barbara E. Walvoord provides helpful information and guidelines for the assessment and improvement of quality in accelerated learning programs. William J. Husson and Tom Kennedy offer in Chapter Five their seasoned insights into creating and maintaining accelerated degree programs in traditional university contexts. To challenge higher education planners who believe that accelerated learning formats can serve only conventional content curriculum, Elise M. Burton in Chapter Six offers the experience and practical knowledge she gained from establishing a distance- and service-learning course within an accelerated format.

The final chapters offer both a critical perspective and a future strategy for a proactive leadership in accelerated learning. Stephen D. Brookfield in Chapter Seven draws on the ideas of Herbert Marcuse and Erich Fromm to examine the controversy of accelerated learning and the specific use of cohort-based accelerated learning. In Chapter Eight, Craig Swenson discusses the future of accelerated learning from the perspective of understanding how effective learning outcomes may be the most important arbiter of quality in higher education. Chapter Nine concludes this volume with a discussion of the future role and influence of accelerated learning in higher education.

Raymond J. Wlodkowski
Carol E. Kasworm
Editors

Reference

Lenzer, R., and Johnson, S. S. "Seeing Things as They Really Are." *Forbes*, Mar. 1997, p. 127.

RAYMOND J. WLODKOWSKI is director of the Center for the Study of Accelerated Learning and professor in the School for Professional Studies at Regis University, Denver.

CAROL E. KASWORM is professor of adult education and department head of Adult and Community College Education at North Carolina State University, Raleigh.

1

This chapter provides a research-based overview of accelerated learning as a program and educational format in higher education today.

Accelerated Learning in Colleges and Universities

Raymond J. Wlodkowski

Accelerated learning programs are one of the fastest-growing transformations in higher education. They are one of the most controversial changes as well, challenging such fundamental academic structures as faculty tenure and the standard forty-five clock hours of instruction. At the Center for the Study of Accelerated Learning, we have identified 250 colleges and universities with specifically identified accelerated programs, the vast majority of these designed to serve adult students. Any postsecondary program targeted for working adults has either started or considered the initiation of an accelerated learning format. Estimates are that 25 percent or more of all adult students will be enrolled in accelerated programs within the next ten years. Currently, 13 percent of adult students studying for degrees are enrolled in programs that offer degrees in less than the traditional length of time (Aslanian, 2001).

The National Center for Education Statistics (2001) reports that 41 percent of students enrolled in degree-granting higher education institutions in fall 1998 were adults. These 6 million students (age twenty-five and older) need a college education to develop their careers and acquire new skills and knowledge in a global society where they are likely to have longer life spans than did workers in the past. In the past twenty years, nontraditional universities such as the University of Phoenix (with more than 130,000 students) have emerged with accelerated learning formats to attract adult learners. Most accelerated programs, however, are found in traditional institutions (at least 200 of them around the country) that have developed these formats specifically to serve working adults.

NEW DIRECTIONS FOR ADULT AND CONTINUING EDUCATION, no. 97, Spring 2003 © Wiley Periodicals, Inc.

In general, adult education is a fast-growing enterprise, especially among faith-based colleges. A national study of church-related schools (mainline Protestant, evangelical Protestant, and Catholic) found that two-thirds of them had instituted one or more bachelor's degree programs for adult students. Sixty percent of these programs had begun in the past thirteen years (Mission, Formation and Diversity Project, 1999), and many of them are now accelerated programs. These schools realized, as Scott and Conrad found in 1992 in their research literature review, that adults appreciate the efficiency of accelerated learning formats. In other words, students valued completing courses and attaining degrees in less time than usual.

Internationally, accelerated learning programs are also rapidly growing. Universities, from the United States or with assistance from organizations within the United States, are featuring this approach in Puerto Rico, the Philippines, Ireland, Germany, and Australia.

Defining an Accelerated Learning Program

By definition, accelerated learning programs are structured for students to take less time than conventional (often referred to as traditional) programs to attain university credits, certificates, or degrees. The core element in accelerated learning programs is the accelerated course. Ground-based (as opposed to on-line) accelerated courses are presented in less time than the conventional number of instructional contact hours (for example, twenty hours of class time versus forty-five hours) and for a shorter duration (for example, five weeks rather than sixteen weeks). Accelerated courses, often referred to as intensive courses (Scott and Conrad, 1992), are usually structured in condensed formats that include weekend and evening classes and workplace programs.

In the case of on-line accelerated courses, the duration of the course may be shorter than conventional standards (eight weeks rather than sixteen weeks), but contact hours are very difficult to calibrate. With instructional configurations such as video streaming, listservs, chatrooms, Internet searches, e-mail, and bulletin boards, the concept of contact hours begins to blur.

With less time formally necessary to achieve credits or degrees, do adult learners in accelerated programs graduate sooner than their peers in conventional programs? One study found that 26 percent of adult students had graduated after three years from an accelerated program in a private college as compared to 18 percent who had graduated in the same time period from a conventional academic program at a public college (Wlodkowski, Mauldin, and Gahn, 2001). After six years, the difference in graduation figures between the two schools had decreased and was no longer significant: 37 percent from the accelerated program and 32 percent from the conventional program. From the perspective of this study, neither accelerated programs nor conventional programs favored degree completion for adult students. Yet a significant percentage of adults did earn their degrees more quickly in the accelerated program.

Why Accelerated Learning Programs Are Controversial

Conventional academics have criticized schools with accelerated programs for stressing convenience over substance and rigor (Wolfe, 1998). They argue that increased contact time is necessary for reflection and analysis of what is being learned. There is also the question of how well instructors can cover the appropriate amount of content in a shortened period of time. Critics regard accelerated courses as being too compressed to produce consistent educational value. They perceive these courses as sacrificing breadth and depth, resulting in learning that is crammed and poorly developed (Shafer, 1995). These critics have referred to universities that use accelerated formats as "McEducation" and "Drive-Thru U." to emphasize their relationship to fast food restaurants and their inferiority to more conventional schools (Traub, 1997).

As Brookfield points out in Chapter Seven in this volume, accelerated programs may represent a commodification of learning in which businesses sell a product (a degree) in a way that undercuts the competition, with students spending less time studying and less time at school. "After all," he writes, "the concern is often to move as many people (paying customers) through a program as quickly as possible, so that more may be recruited into the next cycle."

In addition, accelerated learning programs often do away with such conventional academic accoutrements as tenure, nonprofit status, the semester system, and full-time faculty (Wlodkowski and Westover, 1999). The programs rely on affiliate or adjunct faculty who have full-time jobs apart from the university and usually apply a standardized and predesigned curriculum. In fact, some programs offer a marketing strategy that emphasizes that students will learn from "working professionals." The implication is that these instructors will be more attuned to the realities of today's workplace. Such transparent advertising implicates the irrelevance of the more established "ivory tower" university. In general, these policy differences and marketing campaigns threaten the status quo of conventional academics and probably stimulate their criticism of accelerated learning programs.

Quality of Accelerated Learning Courses and Programs

As in the case of conventional academic programs, we cannot make a general assessment that accurately fits all the accelerated learning programs in higher education. We know immediately that the variety of possibilities is immense and that all programs are not excellent. We also know that the issue of quality in education is a conundrum, a perplexing question rife with the conflicting values, standards, and criteria of scholars and public alike. Following are some of the barometers of quality in higher education that have been applied to accelerated learning programs.

Accreditation. As part of an accredited college, regional accrediting bodies such as the North Central Association of Colleges and Schools assess accelerated learning programs. Although the process of regional accreditation review is not without its critics, it generally affords the public an understanding that an institution that receives accreditation has met acceptable academic standards and has the resources to provide a satisfactory college education. In addition, individual departments within accelerated programs such as management and accounting are eligible for review by national, professional, and specialized accrediting bodies. There is yet no published review of how well accelerated learning programs fare when they submit a particular department or discipline for evaluation by these specific accrediting agencies.

Learning. There remains the strong intuitive notion in higher education that learning is less effective when less than the traditional amount of time is devoted to it. Researchers have studied the relationship between time and learning, but their findings are not clear (Karweit, 1984). Walberg's synthesis (1988) of the time and learning research concluded that time is a necessary but not sufficient condition for learning and that time in and of itself is only a modest predictor of achievement. Depending on the task at hand, other factors that influence learning, as much as or more so than the time spent on learning, are student capability, quality of instruction, and personal motivation (Wlodkowski, 1999). In general, the findings from these studies suggest not allocating fixed amounts of time to learning without consideration of the previously mentioned factors. This generalization is also supported by recent brain research indicating that the neural connections and networks that make up long-term memory (the part of learning that lasts) will fade unless the memory unit is reused or reinforced through application or relationships relevant to one's life (Ratey, 2001).

Recent studies in which researchers compared the learning of younger (traditional) students enrolled in sixteen-week courses with the learning of adult students enrolled in five-week versions of the same courses suggest that accelerated courses provide levels of learning indistinguishable from or greater than those demonstrated by the younger students in conventional courses (Wlodkowski and Westover, 1999; Wlodkowski, Iturralde-Albert, and Mauldin, 2000).

Using summative assessments that required students' demonstration of critical thinking and application of a learned knowledge base, Wlodkowski and Westover (1999) investigated three courses: Accounting II, Business Law, and Introduction to Philosophy. They found that regardless of format, conventional or accelerated, four of five student assessments met a standard of satisfactory to excellent for course work at the college level as judged by three faculty experts in their respective fields of study. In a similar study conducted in Spanish in Puerto Rico, Wlodkowski, Iturralde-Albert, and Mauldin (2000) investigated four courses: Introduction to Economics, History of Puerto Rico, Human Relations in Business, and Labor Relations. They found that the average performance of the older students in the accelerated courses was significantly higher than the average performance of the younger students in conventional courses as rated by three faculty experts in their respective fields of study. Findings from these two modest studies exemplify the possibility that factors such as motivation, concentration, work experience, self-direction, and, paradoxically, an abbreviated amount of time for learning may catalyze learning.

In a more qualitative comparative study, Conrad (1996) found that intensive courses became rewarding and powerful learning experiences when certain attributes were present (see Chapter Three, this volume). These attributes included instructor enthusiasm and expertise (usually gained through experience), active learning, classroom interaction, good course organization, student input, a collegial classroom atmosphere, and a relaxed learning environment. When these attributes were present, the intensive courses allowed for more concentrated, focused learning; more collegial, comfortable classroom relationships; more memorable experiences; more in-depth discussion; less procrastination; and stronger academic performances. When these attributes were missing, writes Scott (Chapter Three, this volume), students reported "intensive courses to be tedious, painful experiences."

Student Attitudes. Historically, college student evaluations of conventional courses generally are positive and indicative of student satisfaction (Astin, 1993). This trend is true for adult student perceptions of accelerated courses and programs as well. The findings of more recent studies (Wlodkowski and Westover, 1999) reflect the findings of the first comprehensive review (Scott and Conrad, 1992) of research assessing accelerated formats. In both, students, especially adults, appreciate their effectiveness and the strong interest they cultivate.

When the perceptions of adult students in accelerated courses are compared with the perceptions of younger students in conventional versions of the same types of courses with the same instructors, both groups generally have positive and similar attitudes toward their courses. These findings noted that both reported valuable learning experiences with positive social climates for peer interaction (Wlodkowski and Westover, 1999). In a qualitative study, Kasworm (2001) found that adults perceived their accelerated degree program to be "a supportive world defined for adult learners" as compared to their previous impersonal and bureaucratic young adult collegiate experiences (see Chapter Two, this volume).

Alumni Attitudes. Another possible indicator of quality is alumni attitude toward accelerated courses. Since alumni have hindsight and experience in the workforce after they have completed their accelerated degree programs, their perceptions are tested by time and their actual work experiences. When alumni attitudes toward the accelerated courses of Management, Human Resource Management, and Corporate Finance were assessed, their perceptions were nearly as positive as those of the current students measured with the same self-report survey as cited above (Wlodkowski and Westover, 1999). These courses were part of their major, and their satisfaction may be related to this fact (Astin, 1993). Nonetheless, these alumni were randomly selected from among eight hundred graduates from the three colleges and represent a broad range of course sections and instructors in accelerated courses.

The Initial Evidence. When the four barometers of quality—accreditation, learning, student attitudes, and alumni attitudes—are considered, the initial evidence is that adults in accelerated programs do learn satisfactorily and in a manner that meets the challenge of conventional college course work. These adults also consistently report a positive outlook toward their accelerated learning experience.

On average, the adult students in the studies cited were fifteen years older and with fifteen years more work experience than the younger students in the conventional courses. These differences may be part of a constellation of characteristics that enable adult students who self-select into accelerated programs to do well in a more abbreviated learning experience. For example, professional work experience probably enhances the writing skills of many adult learners. Report writing in business requires one to organize facts and data into clear and direct narratives. Persistence studies offer insight into some of these characteristics.

Persistence and Success in Accelerated Programs

There is a great deal of research about the persistence and success of traditional-age college students, but few studies focus on adult students, and even fewer attend to adult students in accelerated learning programs. Based on studies at several colleges (Wlodkowski, Mauldin, and Gahn, 2001; Wlodkowski and Westover, 1999), the typical adult student in an accelerated program is a thirty-six-year-old white woman who is married, working full time outside the home, and with more than fifteen years of work experience. Although the range varies widely among individual colleges with accelerated programs, the undergraduate degree completion rate for adult students in the studies cited averages close to 40 percent within six years. Nationally, the six-year graduation rate is 38 percent for undergraduate students, regardless of age, in large urban state colleges and universities (American Association of State Colleges and Universities, 1997).

Researchers (Wlodkowski, Mauldin, and Gahn, 2001; Wlodkowski, Mauldin, and Campbell, 2002) have recently completed a two-year study to identify factors that influence adult students' continuing involvement in course work or graduation (persistence) and grade point average (success).

The study examined two schools: a large faith-based university with an extensive cadre of accelerated programs (enrollment 11,500 adult students) and a public university with an enrollment of 11,000 students with a large adult population primarily in traditional programs.

The researchers used four methods to collect data: (1) a historical analysis to track the records of a cohort of 370 or more adult students at each institution from 1993 to 1999; (2) the Adult Learning Survey (Wlodkowski, Mauldin, and Gahn, 2001) to assess a set of variables among current students that included demographic characteristics, transfer credits, financial aid, and motivation factors; (3) an exit survey to understand the reasons that adults left their respective college; and (4) telephone interviews to more qualitatively understand their experiences prior to withdrawing from college. This study provided the following important findings:

• Adult students benefit from having significant prior college experience before enrolling in four-year colleges, whether in accelerated or conventional programs. Having more transfer credits was associated with degree completion at both schools. Prior college experience may provide some degree of confidence, coping skill, and familiarity with college learning, contributing to successful persistence and degree attainment.

• Adult students with higher grades were more likely to persist and succeed at both institutions. This finding is consistent with conventional wisdom and prior research based on traditional-age students (Astin, 1993).

• Financial aid strengthened adult student persistence at both institutions. At the school with the accelerated program, adults who received financial aid were three times more likely to persist than adults who received no financial aid. For adults in the school with the accelerated program, 50 percent of the students indicated "not enough money to go to school" as a significant reason for leaving, and 46 percent recommended additional financial aid as something their college could do to influence them to continue their enrollment. In this regard, clearly more women than men called for "lower tuition costs" (81 percent versus 41 percent) and "additional financial aid" (60 percent versus 27 percent).

• Lack of time was the dominant theme for leaving both colleges. The adult students repeatedly and emphatically mentioned competing priorities and not having enough time to meet the demands of family, work, and school. Among adults in the school with the accelerated program, the top two reasons for leaving college indicated in the survey were "conflict between job and studies" (60 percent) and "home responsibilities too great" (59 percent).

• At least one-fourth of the students at both schools saw improved guidance and better advising as a positive influence for remaining in school. Misinformation, confusion, and lack of follow-up were major complaints from the students in the accelerated program.

- Women were twice as likely as men to graduate within six years from the school with the accelerated program. The assessments did not shed light on this intriguing finding.
- Better social integration with peers correlates with persistence at both schools. Research findings from other studies confirm that positive involvement with peers and faculty encourages adult students to persist (New England Adult Research Network, 1999; Tinto, 1998).
- A higher percentage of students graduated sooner from the school with the accelerated format. After three years, 26 percent of adult students had graduated from the school with accelerated programs, while 18 percent had graduated from the school with the conventional programs. This finding, although expected, is seldom documented.

As is often the case when studying alternative educational formats, findings from such studies offer implications for both conventional and more radically different educational institutions. It is obvious from this research that there is a need for increased financial aid for adult students, particularly women. Other studies have found that most adult undergraduates rely on personal funds to cover college costs (Aslanian, 2001). Only 20 percent use loans, 19 percent receive grants or scholarships, and 18 percent receive tuition reimbursement. When tuition reimbursement is available, 70 percent of adults use this benefit. Financial sources including federal aid, foundation support, and tuition discounts are areas for new policy development to assist adult students, whether they are in schools with accelerated learning programs or with conventional learning formats.

These findings also support the creation or expansion of weekend course schedules for adults. Weekend courses or programs offer adults, especially women conflicted with job and family responsibilities, more flexibility in finding resources to remain in school. Although less than 10 percent of adults attend weekend courses, nearly half have reported a strong interest in this alternative (Aslanian, 2001). An accelerated program with its intense schedule is likely to make weekend courses a more adaptable choice for adults with family and work priorities.

In general, advising needs to be a more understandable and dependable process for adult students. This is especially so in accelerated programs where the process of course taking and learning moves quickly. During the first year of enrollment, effective advising is crucial. Course selection and sequencing can be critical in making or breaking the confidence of a novice adult student with little college experience.

Finally, deepening positive involvement with peers and faculty continues to encourage adult students to persist. This well-known finding appears to be true for adult students in accelerated programs as well (see Chapters Two and Three, this volume). Peer cohorts and support programs have been instrumental in significantly improving retention in schools with accelerated programs (P. Coffman, personal communication, 2001).

Issues for Further Research

Accelerated learning programs in higher education began about twenty-five years ago. As new and fledgling enterprises, they did not have the resources or time to engage in organized research. Today, most studies in the field of accelerated learning tend to be modest at best. Often, these studies are doctoral dissertations. Only within the past five years has there been an effort to conduct research and share findings in professional associations. The expansion of accelerated learning programs in higher education has far exceeded a rigorous assessment of their context, process, or outcomes.

Most of the studies reported in this chapter are directed toward undergraduate business management programs, probably the most heavily enrolled and attractive accelerated programs nationally. Some of the reasons that business management programs are so popular are that the adult market for them is large and their professional experience transfers to business course work. Also, adjunct faculty can be readily secured from the business sector, with their expertise obvious and relevant to adult students. In addition, business curriculum is relatively uncomplicated and easy to generate into standardized modules. Deepening the appeal of business programs has been a national economy that until recently makes adults hopeful of new and better jobs on graduation. However, research that can more adequately inform the development of accelerated formats throughout other important disciplines in higher education is lacking. In this respect, we need studies directed toward accelerated programs in areas such as the physical and natural sciences and medicine and engineering.

With the exception of the qualitative study by Scott (1996), we have not compared the learning and attitudes of young adult students below the age of twenty-five in accelerated formats with young adult students in conventional formats of the same courses. Researchers have had difficulty finding large enough samples of adults below the age of twenty-five in accelerated courses to make these comparisons. There may be an extensive number of younger adult students who could effectively learn in an accelerated format. This is an important direction for educational policy research.

We also lack research that compares the characteristics and performance of working adults in accelerated formats with working adults in conventional formats of the same courses. Finding large enough samples is again the major hindrance to such studies. Research of this nature could better inform us about the quality of accelerated courses and whether there are significant differences between students who are effective and students who are not effective in accelerated programs. In terms of persistence, the initial evidence is that there are few differences of any significance between adults who attend schools with accelerated programs and those who attend schools with conventional programs.

Studies of adult student persistence and success have just begun. We need to extend studies of this nature to a wider sample of colleges and adult students. With this research, we may identify the structures and processes within colleges that increase adult access and opportunity for degree completion. These studies need to include the tracking of students and a specific understanding of advising procedures, financial aid policies, course sequencing, cohort structures, teaching methods, and motivational influences. Such research will help us to define practices that realistically foster success for adults in accelerated programs as well as in traditional programs.

In higher education, we are in a new world of learning, no longer bound by the conventions of the past. On-line learning, technologically mediated learning, accelerated learning, for-profit as well as nonprofit providers, and a burgeoning adult learner market have transformed higher education. Almost 75 percent of undergraduate students today are considered nontraditional (National Center for Education Statistics, 2002). These students are typically a few years older than most high school graduates, attend college part time, are financially independent, and delay their enrollment into college beyond high school graduation. Given the demands of their jobs and families, they prefer programs that are time efficient and responsive to their needs and lifestyles (Aslanian, 2001).

Colleges with accelerated programs accommodate nontraditional students. Yet these institutions remain challenged by many of the same issues that face traditional universities: how to provide a quality education for all students who attend their schools, how to remain true to their mission, and how to be an agent of equitable social and economic improvement in a global world. Rigorous procedures of self-assessment and research within and between schools with accelerated programs are critical to these purposes. This chapter has described such a beginning in the shadow of a much larger future.

References

American Association of State Colleges and Universities. *Access, Inclusion, and Equity: Imperatives for America's Campuses.* Washington, D.C.: American Association of State Colleges and Universities, 1997.

Aslanian, C. B. *Adult Students Today.* New York: College Board, 2001.

Astin, A. *What Matters in College? Four Critical Years Revisited.* San Francisco: Jossey-Bass, 1993.

Conrad, P. A. "Attributes of High-Quality Intensive Course Learning Experiences: Student Voices and Experiences." *College Student Journal,* 1996, *30,* 69–77.

Karweit, N. "Time-on-Task Reconsidered: Synthesis of Research on Time and Learning." *Educational Leadership,* 1984, *41,* 32–35.

Kasworm, C. "A Case Study of Adult Learner Experiences of an Accelerated Degree Program." Paper presented at the American Educational Research Association Conference, Seattle, Wash., Apr. 2001.

Mission, Formation and Diversity Project. *The Mission, Formation and Diversity Survey Report: Adult Degree Programs at Faith-Based Colleges.* Princeton, N.J.: Center for the Study of Religion at Princeton University, 1999.

National Center for Education Statistics. *Digest of Education Statistics 2000.* Washington, D.C.: U.S. Government Printing Office, 2001.

National Center for Education Statistics. *The Condition of Education 2002*. Washington, D.C.: U.S. Government Printing Office, 2002.

New England Adult Research Network. *Factors Influencing Adult Student Persistence in Undergraduate Degree Programs*. Amherst, Mass.: University of Massachusetts, 1999.

Ratey, J. J. *A User's Guide to the Brain: Perception, Attention, and the Four Theatres of the Brain*. New York: Pantheon, 2001.

Scott, P. A. "Attributes of High-Quality Intensive Course Learning Experiences: Student Voices and Experiences." *College Student Journal*, 1996, *30*(1), 69–77.

Scott, P. A., and Conrad, C. F. "A Critique of Intensive Courses and an Agenda for Research." In J. C. Smart (ed.), *Higher Education: Handbook of Theory and Research*. New York: Agathon Press, 1992.

Shafer, D. W. "A Qualitative Study of Adult and Traditional College Students' Perceptions of a Compressed and Traditional Length College Course." Unpublished doctoral dissertation, Boston University, 1995.

Tinto, V. "Colleges as Communities: Taking Research on Student Persistence Seriously." *Review of Higher Education*, 1998, *21*, 167–177.

Traub, J. "Drive-Thru U.: Higher Education for People Who Mean Business." *New Yorker*, Oct. 20–27, 1997, pp. 114–123.

Walberg, H. J. "Synthesis of Research on Time and Learning." *Educational Leadership*, 1988, *45*, 76–85.

Wlodkowski, R. J. *Enhancing Adult Motivation to Learn: A Comprehensive Guide for Teaching All Adults*. (Rev. ed.) San Francisco: Jossey-Bass, 1999.

Wlodkowski, R. J., Iturralde-Albert, L., and Mauldin, J. *Report on Accelerated Learning Project: Phase 4*. Denver: Center for the Study of Accelerated Learning, Regis University, 2000.

Wlodkowski, R. J., Mauldin, J. E., and Campbell, S. "Early Exit: Understanding Adult Attrition in Accelerated and Traditional Postsecondary Programs." *Synopsis: Higher Education Research Highlights*. Indianapolis: Lumina Foundation for Education, July 2002.

Wlodkowski, R. J., Mauldin, J. E., and Gahn, S. W. *Learning in the Fast Lane: Adult Learners' Persistence and Success in Accelerated College Programs*. Indianapolis: Lumina Foundation for Education, 2001.

Wlodkowski, R. J., and Westover, T. "Accelerated Courses as a Learning Format for Adults." *Canadian Journal for the Study of Adult Education*, 1999, *13*(1), 1–20.

Wolfe, A. "How a For-Profit University Can Be Invaluable to the Traditional Liberal Arts." *Chronicle of Higher Education*, Dec. 4, 1998, pp. B4–B5.

RAYMOND J. WLODKOWSKI is director of the Center for the Study of Accelerated Learning and professor in the School for Professional Studies at Regis University, Denver.

2

Key research has identified adult students' beliefs about the importance of structure, relationships, student identity, and related beliefs about learning, as well as suggesting a conceptual model.

From the Adult Student's Perspective: Accelerated Degree Programs

Carol E. Kasworm

[Why did I select this program?] I know exactly what my class schedule will be from now until the day I graduate. . . . I like to think about it as the closest thing you could come to education, without having to think. You do have to think very hard for class, but you don't have to think of anything else. It enabled me to see the light at the end of the tunnel and that's what I like about it [male student].

It's a fifteen month [program], very rapid; everything is fast paced. Getting my life organized around this program; that was a big factor, I mean even right down to grocery shopping. I even had to change that schedule. And now—all of a sudden—you no longer do your chores whenever you want to; you have to do them around the class. . . . You jump right into it—head first. You're just going full speed ahead from the first class. But starting this program, it just comes right in at once and it was very confusing, a lot of information real fast. And it's a lot to absorb, a lot to comprehend. So probably for the first month, I was really confused. But as time progressed, you get your feet on the ground, and you understand how the system works. You become more comfortable and go from there [female student].

These quotations reflect two students' initial explanations of their experience in an accelerated degree program. Each attempts to explain how this participation was different from his or her earlier enrollment in other collegiate programs. However, these two statements reflect only one layer of many meanings and experiences of these two individuals. Adult students in accelerated degree programs express many complex and diverse understandings based on the structure and focus of the program, their comparative past higher education experiences, and their current adult work, family, and community involvements.

How do we come to understand the adult learner's experience of an accelerated degree program? This chapter presents findings from a qualitative study of the key elements of the adult student's experience of learning and a conceptual model of adult engagement, explaining adult attraction to an accelerated degree program.

The Adult Learning Experience in an Accelerated Degree Program

As the two quotations note, significant adult learner experiences attracted these students and supported learning in the program:

- *Structure*—the supportive learning world of the program
- *Relationships*—the quasi-family relationships with fellow student learners
- *Student identity*—the beliefs of a specific student identity for effective learning and successful completion
- *Adult beliefs regarding learning*—paradoxical beliefs regarding engagement in accelerated degree program learning

These four elements reflect the key landmarks of adult-defined supports and concerns for success through the program. The defining elements were delineated from a qualitative study of twenty adult undergraduate learners in an upper-division applied management accelerated degree program (Kasworm, 2001; Kasworm and Blowers, 1994). Interviewed participants came from different cohort admissions groups and were at various stages of their program, from six months into the program to three months postgraduation. These students stated that their choice for enrollment focused on a convenient, time-bounded, or customized adult learning program. And all noted that this decision had encompassed a range of potential choices, including alternative enrollment at a nearby public or private postsecondary institution. All of the adults had previously experienced at least one other postsecondary environment, if not more, and had entered into the program as an upper-division student. (Further information about the study, sample, and research design are noted in Kasworm, 2001.)

A Supportive Learning World Through an Accelerated Degree Program. Adults in an accelerated degree program believed that they were in a supportive world defined for adult learners. This support was characterized by these adults as (1) an instructional program that was accessible, relevant, and predictable; (2) a degree structure that pushed them through to completion of the degree; and (3) a program that connected them to fellow students in a caring community. These beliefs targeted structures of learning that were adult based, completion based, and community based.

Adults in the accelerated degree program believed they were in a customized learning environment designed for adults. It was easily accessible, given their adult schedules; it offered relevant curricula, practitioner instructors, and part-time involvement with work-oriented instructional focus; and it was systematically preplanned with a publicized lockstep schedule. Unlike their prior experiences of personally negotiated involvements through traditional collegiate programs, they saw this customized program as offering a predictable, adult-friendly, and supportive environment. A number of students defined it as a customer-oriented environment—for example:

> There's very few hassles here. That means, I write a check, and they set down all the books I need for the whole semester, right in front of me. That means, I write a second check, and I have registered and paid for an entire semester, that's it. I park right out front, no parking sticker. I know exactly what my class schedule will be from now until the day I graduate. There's absolutely no question about it.

These adults drew comparisons with previous impersonal, bureaucratic, and time-consuming young adult–oriented collegiate experiences. Furthermore, they noted many aspects of the accelerated degree program that offered supportive resources, scheduling, personnel interactions, and curriculum that directly reflected who they were and how their lives were organized. They believed that the accelerated degree program was designed to fit with their lives, while other collegiate offerings were designed to force adults to fit into a system based on young adult lifestyles and full-time collegiate studies.

Another figural aspect of this supportive world focused on structures and processes that these adults believed locked them into participation and pushed them to completion. As one student noted, "Once you figure out how to make it in the program, you know that you can complete it and graduate. . . . It's all there and planned." What was the basis for this belief of program-designed engagement? In a recent study on adult persistence in accelerated degree programs, Root (1999) noted the key program supports for academic momentum. In his study, the elements of time, mattering, and psychosocial commitments and rewards supported adult student persistence. A combination of forward movement toward a goal across time and space, as well as motive forces for continued movement against inertia and diffuse resistance, was present in adults who completed an accelerated degree program. This academic momentum was believed to be supported through key adult learner strategies in an accelerated degree program of (1) highly detailed degree plans, (2) structured daily lives, (3) prioritization for use of limited time, (4) unstinting class preparation, and (5) adoption of coping attitudes expressed in the phrase, "I can do anything for five weeks."

Students in this study also shared similar beliefs, but they placed more significance on the organization of the program than on individual efficacy. They suggested that the program structure was a type of "Velcro experience" that supported and sustained progress and kept them on track to degree completion (Kasworm, 2001).

A third aspect of this supportive world was a bonding with fellow students in a learning community. Adult students believed that learning occurred in interactions and negotiations with fellow students who were also focused on their work worlds in relation to the degree program. Through engagement with fellow adults who are full-time workers and through use of cohort group projects and cohort-based classes, they experienced a learning community of shared perspectives and applications. More important, these adults felt a sense of support in the midst of their pressured lives. As one student emphasized, "The group is a positive force, because the group demands that you do your homework. It's not a matter of you just letting yourself down, you're letting other people down that you're responsible to" (Kasworm, 2001, p. 6).

Support of Fellow Students as Family. For these adult students, involvement in an accelerated degree program was emotionally intensive and demanding. Beyond these time-intense demands, they also faced unforeseen crises and issues within their other adult roles with their spouse, children, work, friends, and community leadership activities. While participating in the program, most of these adults attempted to make sense of and resolve key crises, tragedies, or conflicts—such as divorce, the death of a parent, drug intervention for a child, downsizing at their work site, or reassignment to a more demanding position. Unlike other prior collegiate programs in which the student was a solo participant, this accelerated degree program offered an admissions model of twelve to twenty students in a cohort program group and class-designated cohort learning groups of approximately three to five members for course case study discussions and projects. These two cohort elements provided a structure, a developed community of practice (Wenger, 1998). They also provided group friendship and intimacy that implicitly supported personal sharing and problem solving, a quasi-family of caring. Adult students noted valuing these groups when faced with life demands beyond their level of resilience. "And over time," noted one student, "they become your support group, and you learn to talk about your fears and your problems and anything that you are having difficulties with in school, as well as out of school with this group of people. And they help you work through things." These students believed that the program provided emotional support and personal connections when handling most of life's challenges: "We have been through each others' pains, personal problems, plus school problems; so, it's almost like a family." These cohort group sharings offered adults a balancing perspective to release anxieties, anger, and fears in a caring friendship group and to provide perspective that their complex lives could be manageable and hopeful.

A Successful Adult Student Identity. Adult students believed that it took a specific kind of adult student for effective learning and persistence in the accelerated degree completion program. Although a variety of adult students were initially attracted to the program, these interviewed adults believe that the identity of a successful student reflected a specific motivation, dedication, and responsibility to the intensive time demands of the accelerated courses and program.

These adult students also suggested that there were four types of students who did not fit this definition and either dropped out the program or barely made it through. The first three types left the program because they were unable or unwilling to adapt to the program structures and demands of accelerated learning involvement. These three groups represented 15 to 30 percent of the entering students of the respective cohort groups. The last type of student, who typically reflected one to two students (10 to 15 percent) of their cohort groups, did not actively engage in the learning process and minimally participated in the program.

These interviewed adult students reported a number of dynamic processes that identified the successful and the unsuccessful students. Students judged not to be successful, as observed by the interviewees, were not able to negotiate a complex set of strategies, attitudes, and beliefs identified as dedication, motivation, and responsibility to the accelerated degree program.

During the first courses after entry into the program, students went through a period of adjustment. Most discovered that they needed to refresh or develop a set of different learning strategies and attitudes to handle the special demands of the program. They could not rely on past strategies that dealt with a slower pace and intermittent engagements with learning activities. The interviewees believed that successful students went through a process of adjustment that refocused their lives, time commitments, and role demands. Successful adult students created a mental life space to do the course work and attend the class sessions, create a new time schedule to keep up with the pace, and rethink their other role commitments in relation to this new and important commitment to the degree program. If adult participants could not adjust to the demands of the course work and could not keep up the pace of learning through the accelerated learning classroom, they dropped out by the end of the second course. (Adults in this program attended one course at a time, with each course lasting approximately four to six weeks in length.) One person noted about these early dropouts, "Not all who want it can do it."

Successful students were able to negotiate a student identity and related skills and attitudes that were congruent with the accelerated degree program. However, the first category of students dropped out of the program because they could not adapt and succeed with the demands and structures of the program. They were unable to handle the time commitments and related learning strategies of the accelerated course work, readings, and papers.

The second and third types of students had brought unrealistic expectations regarding the program that would offer a shorter journey toward a college degree. Specifically, the second type of student dropped out because of inaccurate expectations regarding the demands of the program. Interviewed adults observed that these entering students believed the program would be easy and undemanding but quickly learned that it was not a "slide-through program."

The third type of student was attracted to the program because of the portfolio assessment process and vocalized expectations of rapid accumulation of extra course hours. The interviewed students observed that these students presumed that it would be easy to get the credit hours; they viewed the portfolio process as a short-cut. However, the demands of the process in documentation and written presentation for portfolio assessment were surprisingly difficult and time-consuming for these students. They questioned their key decision to enter the program based on these expectations and often dropped out.

The final type of unsuccessful student learner, as judged by these adult accelerated degree students, was the credential-only student who appeared to be superficially involved in the program. This student type did not actively engage in the homework assignments and appeared to want to get by with minimal work. The interviewed adults held these credential-only students in low regard, avoiding teaming with them in collaborative class work assignments.

Adult Beliefs Regarding Learning in an Accelerated Degree Program. Adult students in accelerated degree programs expressed four paradoxical tensions regarding their learning experiences. The first tension focused on the predictable structure of preset scheduled courses and the program. These adult students specifically sought out the program for its predictable structure, valuing it as supportive and adult oriented. Yet as they approached the midpoint to the end of the program, many reported feelings of constraint by this structure. They wanted individual choice to pursue personal career knowledge needs through self-selected course offerings, an option not available in the program.

A second tension was the contradiction between their attraction to the applied focus of the program and their desire to explore alternative perspectives and ideas at a more conceptual level. Many recognized that the program was designed to aid understanding for the immediate application of knowledge; they noted this applied orientation as extremely relevant to their immediate adult lives and that it was an initial attractor to the program. However, some of the interviewed adults felt that this orientation constrained their growth. They also desired broader understandings and skills to serve them in later roles, to look at their knowledge learning beyond their immediate world. They valued challenges to normative ways of applying knowledge and to assumptions of routine ways of action in the work world.

Most of the adults surfaced a third tension: their strong attraction to the accelerated, fast-tracking degree program with a quicker learning pace, along with their belief that they were not learning with the depth and breadth of knowledge and understanding that had been the case in their slower-paced traditional collegiate experiences. This paradox specifically involved their identity as excellent students, as exemplified by the quality and quantity of their learning. Many suggested that they resolved this tension, in part, by rethinking their desire to be a perfect student—for example, "And I know that there's a lot of people who suffer in our class, thinking that they've got to be the best in everything. . . . And they don't recognize that they don't [need to be the best]. You strive to be the best, but it's not necessary that you are." Thus, many of these adults reported changing their expectations for both grades and their own learning performance. They suggested that they made mental compromises between believing that they should have full and in-depth coverage of the content for their learning in the program versus believing they should do selective learning to keep up with the classes, papers, and exams and the time-compressed demands of the program. To aid them in resolving this tension, most reported that they placed a heavy reliance on the instructors' expertise to select, organize, and effectively present key information. These students believed that the instructors should guide them to learn what was important and in what depth of coverage. In resolving this tension, they valued faculty who had created an accelerated learning environment where they could reasonably meet, given the time constraints, the requirements for the expected learning.

The final tension was between their own beliefs of the value and worth of the accelerated degree program and significant others' expressed beliefs questioning the quality and substance of the program. These adults believed that the accelerated degree program was a godsend, the best learning opportunity for them as adults to this point in their lives. However, they had received judgments by family, friends, or colleagues at work that this accelerated degree program represented a diploma mill, and they questioned the substance of the credential; some colleagues referred to it as a "fluff degree." These adults were angered by and conflicted about these comments; they believed that they were in a quality, demanding program. In fact, they believed their degree was more significant and of higher quality than a traditional collegiate undergraduate degree. Because the accelerated degree focused on both knowledge and applications to learning in the real world of work, they believed that they were gaining a more focused, relevant degree experience. They wanted to prove to their family, friends, and colleagues that these negative judgments were unfounded and demeaning. Yet they lacked the documented evidence to demonstrate the equivalency, if not the superiority, of the degree and their learning. At times, they experienced this tension through self-doubts and concerns that hindered their learning, while they attempted to justify their participation and the quality of the program to others.

These tensions reflected contradictions in the hearts and minds of these adult students and reflected subtexts of their involvement in academic learning. These tensions each uniquely influenced their learning engagement and their reflections on their learning as they progressed through the accelerated degree program.

Adult Engagement in an Accelerated Degree Program: A Model

Now let us consider the initial attractors and motivators uniquely suggested by adults who enrolled in an accelerated adult degree program. The evidence shows that adults entered with external requirements and internal needs shaping their entry, reflecting three distinctive components: adult competence, adult action, and adult work identity (see Figure 2.1).

Adult Competence. Adult students reported attraction to the adult accelerated degree program because it focused on adults as skillful workers and knowledgeable contributors to society. They came to this program because it recognized their competence, provided opportunities for them to demonstrate these knowledge and skills (portfolio assessment), presented an instructional environment linked to their current work efforts, and provided a credential that would attest to and enhance their competence. These adults also noted the explicit press from supervisors and employers for undergraduate credentials that would strengthen their work competence.

An examination and review of the program literature of this adult accelerated degree program, as well as key discussions from the program director, practitioner faculty, and adult students, yielded a background tapestry of structures and processes supporting adult competence. This program presumed that adults brought to the program a rich repertoire of knowledge and skill from prior academic and experiential learning. Course instruction was defined as an active engagement with reflective learning. Thus, new classroom knowledge and skills were often examined and critiqued in relation to past knowledge and past competency. Furthermore,

Figure 2.1. Conceptual Model of an Adult Accelerated Degree Program

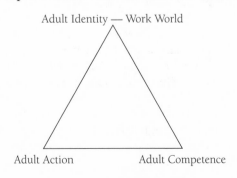

Adult Identity — Work World

Adult Action   Adult Competence

course discussions involved respect and dignity for the adult's existing knowledge and created greater appreciation and new awareness of other beliefs, understandings, and applications.

As part of this grounding support in adult competence, this adult degree program advocated for portfolio assessment of life experiences that could be examined for their equivalency to academic credit. They presumed that adults came into the program with competencies gained beyond the classroom, through workplace training and professional development endeavors. In addition, this program model assumed implicit integration of competence through communities of practice (Wenger, 1998). Through admissions criteria, the program established that the adult must be currently engaged in a full-time work practice. And this accelerated degree program used cohort admissions not only for efficiency but also for synergistic learning engagement of experienced adult workers. The student cohorts stayed together through the length of the program to support and strengthen the students' mutual enhancement of competency. This base in adult competence reflected one of the important elements of a conceptual model of adult engagement in an accelerated degree program.

Adult Action. The accelerated degree program embraced these adult learners' complex world of commitments to action and to learning through those actions. The program situated the adult learner in a convenient, efficient, and accessible program with a structural design and processes that focused on both the adult lifestyles of action and the related competing time demands. For example, the program instructional site was typically close to the work site or within convenient commuting access and parking. The program offered accessible evening or weekend courses, which were preset for the entire length of the program.

Adult students in this study were often overextended in their world of action, with extensive time demands on their life energies and often with competing role priorities. Thus, the program staff and instructional personnel created an adult support system in relation to the adult action world. Registration, books, advising, and other related student systems were designed to serve at times and places convenient for the adults. In addition, the classroom design was based on the belief that these adults needed special support structures and resources that complemented their adult learning processes: for example, cohort groups, active learning strategies, group projects, and practitioner instructors oriented to the adult action world. This action world for adult learning situated perspective development, applications, and critiques within their own work, family, and community lives. Thus, the adult accelerated degree program sought to be both congruent with adult worlds of action and to provide structures and processes to minimize negative effects from this adult world of action that may compete with adult learning environment.

Adult Work Identity. Adults value the accelerated degree programs because they desire advanced career development, targeting key knowledge and skills for improvement of their profession and their workplace. Most accelerated degree programs offered this unique amalgam of basic professional preparation and advanced knowledge of understandings situated in the workplace. The classroom also drew on the student variability of background knowledge and understanding, working with novice to expertise student knowledge along this spectrum. Thus, the class used this diversity to engage minimum levels of knowledge as well as advanced, complex understandings through the active, experiential focus of learning; through class projects and capstone projects focused on work site issues; and with optional assessment of prior life experiences through portfolio development.

Adult students also desired a collegiate program that supported them as they faced challenges in their adult work lives. Baxter Magolda (1999) spoke to the demands and challenges of adult life in relation to the development of self-authorship. She referred to Kegan's work (1994), suggesting that the work world "expects adults to be accomplished masters of their work rather than apprentices, and to be able to look at their work organizations as a whole rather than solely from their own part of the organization. These expectations amount to a demand on the adult mind" (Baxter Magolda, 1999, pp. 264–265). Because adult accelerated degree programs are based on assumptions of learners' maturity and complex life experiences, the instructional and curricular program philosophy values adults who can contextualize their learning and can draw on the demands of their current work situation in relation to the classroom assignments. Thus, adult learners are expected to engage experientially in the learning of ideas. But to meet the demands of their work environments, they need to move beyond memorization of concepts and applications. For some instructors and adult learners, the classroom design provided guidance in the application of content to particular contexts, to consider multiple perspectives and applications for their work world. Some of the adult students noted opportunities to construct new knowledge and understandings in relation to their professional work identities. They were able to engage in self-authorship, to go beyond the information to new understandings.

Finally, this accelerated degree program was designed to integrate key knowledge covered through the courses and assignment projects through the final capstone research action project. These projects were based within the student's work site and reflected both the student's personal inquiry interests and a workplace need. Thus, adult students prior to entry into the program could immediately identify a program philosophy, course offerings, and instructional strategies that supported and enhanced their work identity. And through their program engagements, they were often able to move beyond the theory and concepts to understandings influencing their work identity.

Conclusion

Accelerated degree programs reflect a unique adult-oriented world of learning. Mentkowski and others (2000) noted, "Learning effectively means developing, revising, and depending on mental models about learning" (p. 222). Unlike undergraduate higher educator beliefs of a learning model based on young adults' limited maturity and understandings, adult accelerated degree programs represent a new mental model of learning, grounded in adult maturity and responsible engagement in the world beyond the classroom. These programs combine both program structure and learning designs directed to adult action, adult work identity, and adult competence. They represent learning designs that are adult based, completion based, and community based. These are important new understandings of adult accelerated degree programs and of adult learner involvement and persistence in relationship to these unique programmatic structures and processes.

References

Baxter Magolda, M. B. *Creating Contexts for Learning and Self-Authorship.* Nashville, Tenn.: Vanderbilt University Press, 1999.

Kasworm, C. "A Case Study of Adult Learner Experiences of an Accelerated Degree Program." Paper presented at the American Educational Research Association Conference, Seattle, Wash., Apr. 2001.

Kasworm, C., and Blowers, S. *Adult Undergraduate Students: Patterns of Learning Involvement.* Knoxville: College of Education, University of Tennessee, 1994. (ED 376 321)

Kegan, R. *In over Our Heads: The Mental Demands of Modern Life.* Cambridge, Mass.: Harvard University Press, 1994.

Mentkowski, M., and others. *Learning That Lasts: Integrating Learning, Development, and Performance in College and Beyond.* San Francisco: Jossey-Bass, 2000.

Root, T. L. "Getting There: A Study of Adult Undergraduate Persistence to Graduation in an Adult-Centered Degree Program." Unpublished doctoral dissertation, University of New Mexico, 1999.

Wenger, E. *Communities of Practice: Learning, Meaning, and Identity.* Cambridge: Cambridge University Press, 1998.

CAROL E. KASWORM is professor of adult education and department head of Adult and Community College Education at North Carolina State University, Raleigh.

3

This chapter outlines the best teaching strategies to use in intensive courses to achieve the best possible learning outcomes.

Attributes of High-Quality Intensive Courses

Patricia A. Scott

Intensive courses have become a mainstay of higher education. Defined as semester- or quarter-equivalent classes offered in compressed, accelerated, or condensed formats, most colleges and universities now offer intensive classes alongside traditional semester-length classes. Although intensive courses have become quite common, many academic and administrative pundits condemn their use and claim that these formats sacrifice academic rigor and learning for student convenience and higher enrollments. Although they offer little research to support their claims, many colleges and universities continue to schedule classes based on assumptions and tradition rather than solid empirical evidence.

Recent research, however, suggests that intensive course formats can be effective alternatives to traditional formats. Scott and Conrad's review (1992) of the intensive course research and studies published since their review (Caskey, 1994; Wlodkowski and Westover, 1999) indicate that intensive courses yield equivalent, and sometimes superior, learning outcomes when compared to matched traditional-length courses. Moreover, under some conditions, intensive courses can lead to a more rewarding learning experience for students than traditionally scheduled classes (Scott and Conrad, 1992; Scott, 1995, 1996).

This chapter explores how students experience intensive courses differently than they do traditional scheduling formats and the factors that contribute to high-quality intensive course experiences. These insights emanate from a qualitative study (Scott, 1994) that compared two matched sets of college classes: an intensive and a semester-length English and marketing class. Each set of classes was taught by the same instructor and

NEW DIRECTIONS FOR ADULT AND CONTINUING EDUCATION, no. 97, Spring 2003 © Wiley Periodicals, Inc.

covered the same material; the only differences were the scheduled formats. The study incorporated participant observation, focused in-depth interviews, and videotaped class session analysis to examine students' experiences and behavior in these classes. The insights resulting from the study help us to understand how to structure intensive courses to maximize their strengths and students' learning.

Attributes of High-Quality Learning Experiences

Based on student interviews and classroom observations, qualitative analysis suggests that students experience intensive classes differently than they do traditional-length courses, but the quality of the experience depends on the presence or absence of certain attributes, which can be grouped into four major categories: instructor characteristics, teaching methods, classroom environment, and evaluation methods. When these attributes are present, students prefer intensive over traditional-length classes for reasons that will be discussed. When these attributes are absent, most students said intensive courses become boring, painful experiences.

Instructor Characteristics. Students consistently indicated that the instructor was the most essential component to a high-quality intensive course learning experience. They wanted instructors to display certain characteristics.

Enthusiasm. Students relished intensive course instructors who exhibited enthusiasm, even passion, for the subject and for teaching. Students mentioned that instructor enthusiasm was infectious and motivated them to commit more energy to learning; it also made the course seem more important and meaningful.

Knowledge, Experience, and Good Communication. Students appreciated intensive course instructors who demonstrate expertise on the subject through their knowledge and, most important, experience. Although instructors often possess the necessary knowledge, many students perceived instructors to lack meaningful experience. Students wanted instructors to "bring the subject to life" and explain the subject's relevance, which more likely occurred when the instructor had "lived" the subject. Moreover, instructors needed the communication skills to convey that expertise in an understandable and interesting fashion. Students complained that too often, instructors talk above them and alienate them from the learning experience.

Willingness to Learn from and Consult with Students. Students wanted intensive course instructors who would step out of their expert role of authority in the classroom and become fellow learners. They admired instructors who "get in the dirt" and "grapple with the material" along with students, as well as instructors who are open-minded, respect students' opinions and experience, do not interject personal biases, and allow themselves to learn from students. For example, when describing a favorite instructor, one student mentioned that the instructor "not only encouraged students' ideas" but would jot down these ideas and use them in other classes. Similarly, students encouraged instructors to consult with them on course-related issues such as the course outline, course expectations, assignments, and course content. Allowing input gave students a sense of control in intensive courses and increased their sense of ownership.

Student Orientation. Instructors can strengthen students' learning experiences in intensive courses by caring about and relating to each student in a class. Students believed that their attitudes about learning improved if instructors "showed they cared" and emphasized the importance of student learning to class success. According to the students interviewed, too many instructors viewed the student-teacher relationship as superfluous, which made students feel insignificant and unimportant.

Teaching Methods. In addition to certain instructor characteristics, students wanted instructors to use what they considered to be effective teaching strategies. Generally, students urged instructors to demonstrate classroom creativity by incorporating a variety of teaching methods to maintain student motivation and interest. Without creativity and variety, students indicated that intensive courses easily become monotonous. Specifically, students highly recommended using active learning methods and emphasizing depth over breadth of learning to enhance the overall experience.

Active Learning. Students unanimously identified active learning as essential to intensive courses. As one student noted, "I don't think the pure lecture with five minutes of questions at the end of class is going to work in the intensive format." Instead, students wanted to engage the material actively.

Learning research supports students' desire for active learning. Learning depends on the degree to which students build meaningful connections between new information and their prior knowledge and experiences. As Wittrock (1987) notes, students do not come to the classroom as blank slates. They arrive with a plethora of knowledge and experiences that support their personal understandings of life and the world around them. To learn successfully, students "must generate connections between the information [they]. . . . are trying to learn and the knowledge already organized in [their]. . . . memory" (Weinstein and Meyer, 1991, p. 16). The more connections students generate, the more meaningful the connections are to them. And the more active the learner is in building these connections, the greater is the likelihood that students will remember and be able to access new information. Students recommended several ways to introduce active learning in the classroom.

Classroom Interaction and Discussion. Students advised instructors to promote classroom interaction primarily through small and large group discussions. According to students, interaction augmented their interest in the subject and facilitated learning by allowing them to verbalize their opinions or understanding of the subject.

Research supports the use of discussion as a classroom strategy. McKeachie, Pintrich, Lin, and Smith (1987) reviewed the teaching and learning literature and concluded, "In those experiments involving measures of retention of information after the end of a course, measures of transfer of knowledge to new situations, or measures of problem solving, thinking, attitude change, or motivation for further learning, the results tend to show differences favoring discussion methods over lecture" (p. 81).

Experiential and Applied Learning. Students advised intensive course instructors to avoid lectures when possible. As one student stated, "I know a lot of classes where students are lectured at, and I don't think that's a very good idea . . . simply because I don't think students' brains are to be poured full of information." Instead, students wanted to experience the material and recommended that instructors incorporate experiential teaching methods such as problem solving, role playing, simulation exercises, field trips, and skill-training practice into the class. Moreover, they wanted to apply the material in addition to experiencing it. For example, many students voiced the desire to personalize the material by applying it to their own lives. Said one student, "You get so much information that you memorize, you lose half of it, whereas the stuff you can remember is stuff that personally plays a part [in your life]."

Once again, research supports students' desire for experiential learning. Research on experiential teaching methods indicates that these approaches appear to optimize student learning better than more passive methods like lectures (Combs and Bourne, 1989; Whiteman and Nielsen, 1986). As McKeachie, Pintrich, Lin, and Smith (1987) concluded, the use of "cases, simulations, and games involve getting, recalling, and using information to solve problems involves the kind of restructuring that should be likely to result in better retention, recall, and use of learning outside the classroom" (p. 89).

Although students preferred experiential and applied learning, they also desired a limited amount of lecture so they could benefit from the instructor's expertise. On these occasions, students advised instructors to infuse examples throughout the lecture, preferably from personal experience. They also recommended the use of demonstrations, thought-provoking questions, and controversial statements to enhance lectures. One student recalled a favorite instructor who once stated, "Today I'm going to try to prove to you that there's no difference between males and females." Controversial statements piqued students' interest and encouraged them to scrutinize the instructor's lecture.

Depth over Breadth: Course Organization. Students believed that organization was one of the most important factors to successful intensive courses. Because intensive courses progress so quickly, instructors need to be organized and present the material in an easy-to-follow manner. Without organization, intensive courses quickly become overwhelming and chaotic. Moreover, students recommended that instructors organize intensive courses to emphasize depth over breadth of learning. Too often, students said, intensive course instructors try to cover too much material, which creates information overload. Students preferred to delve into fewer areas in more depth and concentrate on major concepts rather than learning large amounts of seemingly inconsequential information.

There may be some research to support students' request for depth over breadth of learning. Cognitive science research suggests that learning depends on the depth to which students process new information (Marton and Saljo, 1976). Deep processors—students who take the time to understand new material—recall information significantly better than do surface processors, who merely reproduce or memorize new material. Helping students process new information by emphasizing in-depth learning could result in stronger long-term retention of learned material.

Classroom Environment. In addition to certain instructor characteristics and teaching methods, students noted the importance of a good classroom environment to the success of intensive courses. Students identified classroom relationships, classroom atmosphere, class size, and the physical environment as the most important elements of the classroom environment.

Classroom Relationships. Students advised intensive course instructors to foster close student-student and student-teacher relationships to increase the level of trust and participation. One student recalled that she particularly enjoyed one intensive class because of the instructor, who made a sincere effort to build classroom relationships. As a result, she said, she "felt so at home" and "one-on-one with everyone" that it made the learning experience particularly meaningful to her.

Research indicates that learning, achievement, and retention seem to be socially rooted and that strong classroom relationships with both the instructor and fellow students facilitate student satisfaction and learning outcomes (Billson and Tiberius, 1991). With regard to student-teacher relationships, there is strong evidence that meaningful student-faculty connections positively and significantly contribute to student development, academic achievement, persistence, and educational aspirations in higher education (Pascarella and Terenzini, 1991). As Tiberius and Billson (1991) note in their review of the literature, "Students who are positively connected with their teachers are more likely to feel involved in their educational experience, to be committed to the institution, to have passing grades, and to persist to graduation" (p. 69). Similarly, strong peer relationships also increase student satisfaction and learning outcomes. Wulff, Nyquist, and Abbott's survey (1987) of eight hundred college students found that students identified other students as the second most important factor to their learning, after the instructor.

Atmosphere. Students noted that good intensive course learning experiences require a relaxed classroom atmosphere that encourages student participation. A relaxed atmosphere requires a class size of no more than ten to thirty students and a comfortable physical environment. Students also recommended that instructors "joke around . . . with the class," "chat with students before class," and alter the traditional seating arrangement so students face one another when talking. Most important, the instructor must establish a supportive, nonjudgmental atmosphere. As one student stated, "I've always . . . been a passive learner. . . . I [would] like to be a really hard-hitting participant. In order to do that, I need a teacher who's going to be able to interact [with me] . . . without criticism, without any negativity at all."

Research indicates that learners respond to the entire sensory context in which learning occurs. Consequently, the learning environment is an important variable in the learning process (Caine and Caine, 1991). Although much of the research in this area has been conducted in primary and secondary classrooms, studies have consistently found a relationship between the classroom environment and various cognitive and affective outcomes. Haertel, Walberg, and Haertel's meta-analysis (1981) of the relationship between classroom psychosocial environments and student outcomes concluded that students who perceived their classrooms as cohesive, comfortable, goal directed, organized, and less divisive achieved more than those who did not. The studies conducted in college classrooms reached similar conclusions (Johnson, Johnson, and Smith, 1991).

Evaluation. Students believed that intensive courses require different types of assignments and exams than semester-length classes do. With regard to assignments, students advised instructors to redesign assignments or give "smaller assignments" so they can be readily accomplished within a shorter time frame. Moreover, instructors should choose assignments carefully based on the course objectives and not overload the students with homework. According to those interviewed, students needed time to synthesize learning, and busywork interfered with this objective. Students preferred meaningful assignments that require them to apply or experience the material personally. Some other student recommendations included giving students options on assignments and incorporating more in-class group assignments.

With regard to exams, students rejected objective exams because they encourage cramming. Instead, they advised instructors to use essay exams, which allowed them to demonstrate their knowledge better; take-home exams, which gave them time to communicate what they have learned; or frequent quizzes. Moreover, some students recommended using forms of evaluation other than exams, such as written papers, hands-on projects, and class presentation.

The Consequences of High-Quality Attributes and Intensive Course Scheduling

Students reported that when most of these high-quality attributes were present, intensive courses became rewarding and sometimes powerful learning experiences for a variety of reasons.

Focused Learning. Students felt that successful intensive courses engendered focused, uninterrupted learning. Unlike semester-length classes that students take concurrently with three to four other classes, students often took only one or two intensive courses at a time. Consequently, they felt that under ideal conditions, they synthesized the material better since they could focus on a particular class, uninterrupted by other subjects. This exclusive attention allowed them to immerse themselves in the subject and develop a stronger relationship with the material. During the traditional semester, students had to divide their attention among five subjects.

One additional benefit of this focused learning was that students did not give short shrift to classes that they considered less important (for example, general studies courses). Many students remarked that during the semester, their courses competed for their attention, and they felt forced to prioritize subjects. The courses they viewed as less important often received little or none of their attention. Under intensive course schedules, they could give each course relatively equal attention.

Another benefit of focused learning is that students often experienced a greater sense of control over their schedule. They said that semester schedules were often chaotic and required them to juggle too many responsibilities simultaneously. Conversely, intensive formats permitted them to concentrate on one or two classes exclusively, which allowed them to manage their time better.

More In-Depth Discussions. When the high-quality attributes were present, students also preferred intensive courses because they tended to promote more classroom interactions and in-depth discussions than typical semester-length classes did. One student noted, "This may sound crazy, but I think I liked having three-hour [class sessions] . . . because I think you can really get into something without the class ending." Moreover, students felt there was less downtime in intensive courses. One student said that in semester classes, "you spend fifteen minutes of class trying to get going" and "then you have to spend fifteen minutes trying to wrap up." In intensive courses, students were less likely to hear, "We can't get into this today because we don't have enough time."

Emphasis on Core Concepts. Students generally appreciated that intensive courses required instructors to eliminate what students considered "extraneous material" and stress the most important concepts. These modifications helped students concentrate on the most important material.

More Memorable Learning Experience. As a result of the factors detailed above, students often felt that intensive courses engendered a more memorable learning experience that affected them longer than traditional-length classes. As one student stated:

> I think that a lot of the way that people learn and retain information is directly related to how intense the experience is while they're learning it. If I have an experience that's not particularly intense, that's spread out over a

long period of time, at no point . . . will I have a lot of my mind into it. I really won't have a devotion to the subject or to the material. . . . I remember things that affect me intensely, and because this class for a period of six or eight weeks was a really big part of my life, and it was something that I was thinking about all the time, I think that will always occupy a space in my brain.

Classroom Relationships. Students enjoyed the more collegial relationships they formed in successful intensive courses. Because of their concentrated nature and the increased classroom interaction, intensive formats allowed students to form deeper classroom relationships, which resulted in a greater degree of comfort, camaraderie, and classroom community. One student commented on the closer relationship she formed with one of her intensive course instructors: "I think maybe seeing her every day and seeing that she had personal tragedies and traumas too, you know you probably wouldn't see if you were only going to class a couple days a week [was important]. It made her seem more human and more real."

Classroom Atmosphere. Many students described successful intensive courses as more laid back and informal than semester-length classes even though the class progressed through the material faster. They appreciated instructors' willingness to deviate from traditional teaching practices and engage in dialogue more with students, which created a more relaxed classroom atmosphere and learning environment. One student noted, "When the barriers are brought down between students and between the professor, I think everyone works better and talks better and can be a little more open to ask questions or to bring up situations."

Performance. Most important, students felt their academic performance improved in successful intensive courses compared to semester-length classes due to a number of factors:

• Because students typically took fewer courses in conjunction with intensive courses, they were able to direct their efforts more fully to the intensive course. Said one student, "You were constantly studying this stuff, and you knew that with the final only being three weeks away . . . you didn't forget it. . . . You didn't have to go back and re-learn it all."

• Students maintained their stamina better in intensive courses compared to semester-length classes because of their short duration. Students likened the learning experience to a sprint versus a marathon.

• Because of their short duration and concentrated nature, students felt they retained information and synthesized concepts better compared to semester-length classes. According to this student, "You learned it all at once," so "it's all up there and you can relate it." As a result, students felt that concentrated learning experiences led to greater understanding of the material and more in-depth, creative thinking.

• Students did not procrastinate in their intensive courses as much as they did in their semester-length classes because of their short duration. As a result, they were often better prepared for class discussions and exams compared to their semester-length classes.

Conclusion

There are benefits of intensive courses and students' preference for concentrated learning formats when certain instructional and classroom attributes are present. Students repeatedly indicated that instructor enthusiasm and experience, active learning, classroom interaction, good course organization, student input, collegial classroom atmosphere, and a relaxed learning environment were essential to learning in intensive courses. This chapter also pointed to the supportive research that corroborates the effectiveness of many of the attributes students identified. When these attributes are present, students report that intensive classes allow for the following attributes:

• More concentrated, focused learning
• More collegial, comfortable classroom relationships
• More memorable experiences
• More in-depth discussion
• Less procrastination
• Stronger academic performances

When these attributes are missing, students report intensive courses to be tedious, painful experiences.

This study suggests the importance of using nontraditional instructional practices when teaching intensive courses, but I suspect that many intensive course instructors are not doing so. As Astin (1991) found in his last national survey of college faculty, more than 60 percent of university professors still lecture extensively in all or most of their courses. Lecture corresponds to the transmission model of teaching, which requires instructors to disseminate their "wisdom" to students as if they were empty receptacles (Johnson, Johnson, and Smith, 1991). Although additional research is needed, this study suggests that the expansion of nontraditional scheduling formats must coincide with adoption of alternative teaching practices that will maximize the strengths of these concentrated formats and student learning. Without adoption of these high-quality attributes, instructors may be diminishing student learning and motivation rather than enhancing them.

References

Astin, A. W. *Assessment for Excellence: The Philosophy and Practice of Assessment and Evaluation in Higher Education.* New York: Macmillan, 1991.

Billson, J. M., and Tiberius, R. G. "Effective Social Arrangements for Teaching and Learning." In R. J. Menges and M. D. Svinicki (eds.), *College Teaching: From Theory to Practice.* New Directions for Teaching and Learning, no. 45. San Francisco: Jossey-Bass, 1991.

Caine, R. N., and Caine, G. *Making Connections: Teaching and the Human Brain.* Alexandria, Va.: Association for Supervision and Curriculum Development, 1991.

Caskey, S. R. "Learning Outcomes in Intensive Courses." *Journal of Continuing Higher Education,* 1994, *42*(2), 23–27.

Combs, H. W., and Bourne, G. "The Impact of Marketing Debates on Oral Communications Skills." *The Bulletin,* 1989, *52*(21), 25.

Haertel, G. D., Walberg, H. J., and Haertel, E. H. "Socio-Psychological Environments and Learning: A Quantitative Synthesis." *British Educational Research Journal,* 1981, *7*(1), 27–36.

Johnson, D. W., Johnson, R. T., and Smith, K. A. *Active Learning: Cooperation in the College Classroom.* Edina, Minn.: Interaction Book Company, 1991.

Marton, F., and Saljo, R. "On Qualitative Differences in Learning: II—Outcome as a Function of the Learner's Conception of the Task." *British Journal of Educational Psychology,* 1976, *46*, 115–127.

McKeachie, W. J., Pintrich, P. R., Lin, Y., and Smith, D. A. *Teaching and Learning in the College Classroom: A Review of the Research Literature (1986) and November 1987 Supplement.* Ann Arbor, Mich.: National Center for Research to Improve Postsecondary Teaching and Learning, 1987. (ED 314 999)

Pascarella, E. T., and Terenzini, P. T. *How College Affects Students: Findings and Insights from Twenty Years of Research.* San Francisco: Jossey-Bass, 1991.

Scott, P. A., "A Comparative Study of Students' Learning Experiences in Intensive and Semester-Length Courses and of the Attributes of High-Quality Intensive and Semester Course Learning Experiences." Unpublished doctoral dissertation, University of Wisconsin, 1994.

Scott, P. A. "Learning Experiences in Intensive and Semester-Length Classes: Student Voices and Experiences." *College Student Journal,* 1995, *29*(2), 207–213.

Scott, P. A. "Attributes of High-Quality Intensive Course Learning Experiences: Student Voices and Experiences." *College Student Journal,* 1996, *30*(1), 69–77.

Scott, P. A., and Conrad, C. F. "A Critique of Intensive Courses and an Agenda for Research." In J. C. Smart (ed.), *Higher Education: Handbook of Theory and Research.* New York: Agathon Press, 1992.

Tiberius, R. G., and Billson, J. M. "The Social Context of Teaching and Learning." In R. J. Menges and M. D. Svinicki (eds.), *College Teaching: From Theory to Practice.* New Directions for Teaching and Learning, no. 45. San Francisco: Jossey-Bass, 1991.

Weinstein, C. E., and Meyer, D. K. "Cognitive Learning Strategies and College Teaching." In R. J. Menges and M. D. Svinicki (eds.), *College Teaching: From Theory to Practice.* New Directions for Teaching and Learning, no. 45. San Francisco: Jossey-Bass, 1991.

Whiteman, V. L., and Nielsen, M. "An Experiment to Evaluate Drama as a Method for Teaching Social Work Research." *Journal of Social Work Education,* 1986, *3*, 31–42.

Wittrock, M. C. "Teaching and Student Thinking." *Journal of Teacher Education,* 1987, *38*(6), 30–33.

Wlodkowski, R. J., and Westover, T. N. "Accelerated Courses as a Learning Format for Adults." *Canadian Journal for the Study of Adult Education,* 1999, *13*(1), 1–20.

Wulff, D. A., Nyquist, J. D., and Abbott, R. D. "Students' Perceptions of Large Classes." In M. G. Weimer (ed.), *Teaching Large Classes Well.* New Directions for Teaching and Learning, no. 32. San Francisco: Jossey-Bass, 1987.

PATRICIA A. SCOTT is associate professor of social work at Missouri Western State College, St. Joseph.

Assessment can be used to improve student learning in accelerated programs.

Assessment in Accelerated Learning Programs: A Practical Guide

Barbara E. Walvoord

This chapter is a practical guide for faculty and administrators of programs in accelerated learning, particularly as they work toward self-improvement and they address accreditors, employers, and potential students. The goal of assessment for accelerated learning programs is nearly identical to that of traditional programs. Although accelerated programs serve primarily adult students over the age of twenty-five and use a shorter time frame for learning, their goal remains to provide an excellent education at a college level of challenge for all students. In this respect, this chapter helps practitioners answer the following questions:

- Student performance: Are students in accelerated programs performing as the program or faculty hope? What are students' strengths and weaknesses?
- Relationship between performance and other factors: What is the relationship between the quality of student performance and other factors, such as students' backgrounds or the program's curriculum?
- Improving student performance: How can faculty and programs use the findings on student performance and the relationship between performance and other factors to improve student performance in accelerated learning?

Although research on students in accelerated learning programs can be very helpful, local programs and faculty need assessment strategies that help them answer these assessment questions for their own students. Moreover, it may not be possible to wait for funded research or for the ideal research design. What is needed is action research, defined as research on student learning undertaken as responsibly as possible with the knowledge, time, and resources available, in order to inform decisions for future learning. Such research supplies indicators about where successes and failures may lie. This information suggests strategies that might work to improve the situation. Claims based on such research must fully recognize its limitations. However, the assumption is that for decision making, some evidence, if systematically gathered and thoughtfully interpreted, is better than no evidence. This chapter provides reliable and feasible assessment strategies for faculty and accelerated programs to address the needs identified in the questions already set out.

Defining the Research Question

Do not let the demand for an assessment plan for external accreditation or internal review catapult you into a premature focus on the data you will collect (for example, "We'll do assessment by portfolios"). Rather, approach assessment as a combination of political action and academic research. As you would for any other political action, ask, "Who needs to know what, for what?" Collect only the information that will be well used, and present it in a format for audience use. One frequent mistake is to assume that accreditors want to know how well students are doing, when actually they want to know that *you* know how well your students are doing. And they also want to know that you have ongoing efforts to improve students' learning.

Also, approach assessment as you would any other academic research. Begin with a careful definition of the research question. Here are some examples:

"Are the students in this program [or class] graduating with the knowledge and skills we want? If not, where are they weak?"
"Since I began responding to their drafts, are students in my classes writing better analytical papers?"
"What changes take place in students' quantitative reasoning between the beginning and the end of our program?"

The aspect of student performance you investigate may be fairly broad (for example, quantitative reasoning, designing research in the field, writing analytical papers, dealing with unexpected complications in a nursing situation, acknowledging alternative points of view) or more specific (for example, handling the past tense in Spanish conversation or solving a certain kind of mathematical problem). The broader aspects will require subcategories of analysis. For example, if you are investigating students' ability to write analytical papers, you will be examining their papers for the quality of the analysis, the sufficiency of their support for their analysis, the organization of their papers, and so on. Because each additional aspect requires more work, ask yourself whether your purposes would be served equally well by measuring

Table 4.1.   A Format for Defining Learning Goals

Learning Goal	Measures	Use of Information
Describe basic biological information and concepts	Standardized test given to all seniors *and/or* final exams of three basic biology courses required of all majors	Annually, the standardized exam committee and the teachers of the three basic courses report the test and exam results to the department. At this annual meeting, the department discusses strengths and weaknesses and takes appropriate actions, such as changes in curriculum or asking the math department to serve biology students a bit differently. Meeting outcomes are reported to the dean or other body that has resources to address problems.
Use the scientific method for original research and communicate results to peers, orally and in writing	In senior capstone course, students complete an original scientific experiment, write it up in scientific report format, and make an oral report to the class. The teacher uses a set of explicit criteria to evaluate their work (see Exhibit 4.1).	Annually, the senior capstone teachers share students scores with the department. The department (1) encourages and supports, in collegial ways, classroom change planned by the teacher; (2) takes whatever departmental action is needed; and (3) reports the results to the dean or other body that has resources if needed to address problems.

a more limited set of aspects. For example, you may decide that instead of analyzing all aspects of an analytical paper, you will evaluate only the quality of the analytical claims and evidence.

In external accreditation and internal review situations, the research question frequently is, "Are students in this program achieving the most important knowledge and skills we want?" Defining the most important skills begins when the program or department states its learning goals in this format: "By the time they graduate from this program, we want students to be able to . . . " (see the left column of Table 4.1).

How does a department or program arrive at learning goals? Begin by consulting existing documents and practices. Is there a program or departmental mission statement? Some national professional organizations have constructed goals for student achievement. Another strategy is to ask the faculty in the program to submit the learning goals they have for each course they teach; then a program committee integrates those goals into a statement that is brought to program faculty for their review.

Choosing an Instrument to Evaluate Student Performance

The next task is to select or construct one or more instruments to measure the quality of students' performance in the aspect you are investigating. The measure, which can be direct or indirect, should be quantifiable, specific, and diagnostic, so that you can tell how well students are doing and in what areas.

Direct Measures of Student Performance. Direct measures consist of one or more actual student performances (such as an exam, paper, project, or interaction with a client), directly observed, and evaluated by a set of specific criteria. Grades are a quantifiable measure of student performance, but to say that the class average grade was 3.2 is not sufficiently specific to tell the teacher or the program what to work on. The grading process can be useful if it yields diagnostic information.

The first task in a direct measure is to select or construct a student performance that will demonstrate the aspect of performance you want to investigate. Classroom work and assignments (exams, papers, and projects) are often the best measures because they matter to students, they are already being done, and they take place within the educational process. Classroom work can be the basis of assessment for a program or major, as well as for a single course, as long as the results are shared with the department or program for action at that level.

Instead of, or in addition to, classroom work, a program or department may construct a separate test for its students. For example, faculty in one biology department decided that they would test all seniors for their ability to use certain laboratory equipment. Some disciplines have standardized tests that may be useful, or students may be required to take a qualifying or licensure exam whose results will be reported to the program. Such results are most helpful if they report areas of strength and weaknesses rather than merely the percentage of students who passed.

Issues of validity and reliability are important in choosing a student performance. Validity means that the student performance is actually testing what it purports to test. Examine not only the assignment or test itself but also how students perceive it and how they work on it. For example, a business professor wanted to use his class's term papers to assess their creative problem solving. However, when he asked students to submit their notes and drafts and asked a colleague to interview a sample of his students about how they did their term papers, he found that the term paper was actually demonstrating students' ability to locate, combine, and paraphrase sources. He needed to reframe the assignment and his instructions and to provide better in-process guidance so students attempted the performance he wanted to measure.

Reliability means that the measure of student performance consistently measures the same behavior. For example, when two different projects in an accelerated course require written tasks, each requires the student to demonstrate the same skill: coherent organization of complex thinking. If one of these projects does not require "coherent organization of complex thinking," the two projects are inconsistent in measuring this skill and therefore are unreliable measures of the skill. To achieve reliability in direct measures of student performance, criteria are needed.

Exhibit 4.1.   Sample Primary Trait Scale

Assignment: Semester-long assignment in Biology capstone course: to design an original experiment, carry it out, and write it up in scientific report format.

Traits to measure: Title, Introduction, Scientific Format, Materials and Methods, Nonexperimental Information, Experimental Design, Operational Definitions, Control of Variables, Charts and Graphing, Data Collection, and Interpretation of Data.

Scale Describing Levels of Student Performance for Interpreting Data: Drawing Conclusions/Implications

Rating

5—Student summarizes the purpose and findings of the research; student draws inferences that are consistent with the data and scientific reasoning and relates these to interested audiences; student explains expected results, offers explanations for unexpected results, and/or suggests further research; student presents data honestly, distinguishes between fact and implication, and avoids overgeneralizing; student organizes nonexperimental information to support conclusion; student accepts or rejects the hypothesis.

4—As 5 above, but the student does not accept or reject the hypothesis.

3—As 4 above, but the student overgeneralizes and/or fails to organize nonexperimental information to support conclusions.

2—The student summarizes the purpose and findings of the research; explains expected results but ignores unexpected results.

1—The student may or may not summarize the results, but fails to interpret their significance to interested audiences.

Direct measures also require that the performance be rated against a set of criteria specific enough to be diagnostic. Looking at a student paper and saying, "Well, it feels like a B," may be an accurate assessment based on the instructor's tacit knowledge, but if the assessment is to be diagnostic and usable by others, the unidentified criteria behind the judgment of a grade of B have to be articulated. The technique of primary trait analysis offers a way to construct specific criteria (see Exhibit 4.1). (For a fuller discussion about how to construct primary trait analyses in various disciplines, see Walvoord and Anderson, 1998.)

Once you have chosen one or more performances and have articulated specific criteria, you are ready to analyze the data. If the performance is classroom work, analysis may be conducted by the instructor or by a group of colleagues. One biology department used students' final research projects in their capstone course to assess their ability to conduct original scientific research (as shown in Table 4.1). The teacher of the capstone course constructed a set of specific criteria (shown in Exhibit 4.1). She evaluated the papers herself against the criteria as part of her grading process. However, she also brought aggregated data annually to the department (see Table 4.2), so they could monitor their graduating majors' skills in such areas as designing research and interpreting data. The teacher might say to the department, "I tried several new teaching methods, and as you can see, student scores have improved. I'll need a few more semesters to see whether the improvement holds up. However, I'm not satisfied with their ability to construct

Table 4.2.   Example of Aggregated Data for a Biology Class

Trait	Class Mean, Last Spring	Class Mean, Current Spring
Title	2.95	3.22
Introduction	3.18	3.64
Scientific format	3.09	3.32
Materials and methods	3.00	3.55
Nonexperimental information	3.18	3.50
Charts and graphing	2.42	2.49
Experimental design	2.68	3.32
Operational definitions	2.68	3.50
Control of variables	2.73	3.18
Data collection	2.86	3.36
Interpretation of data	2.90	3.59
Overall	2.88	3.33

Note: The data are aggregated on a scale of 1 to 5. For interpretation, see Exhibit 4.1.

graphs and charts, and I don't think we ought to be teaching graphing in the senior capstone. Is there a place earlier in the curriculum where we can do more intensive instruction in graphing?" This instructor's report can lead to a departmental discussion about how to address graphing skills better.

Relying on the teacher's report is an efficient method because the teacher is conducting assessment for the grading as well, and student work is scored only once. However, it is also possible to collect wider input for establishing criteria or scoring student work. For example, the department as a whole or all the instructors who teach a particular course might together establish the criteria to be used for students' final projects. Also, the department might ask several of its members, or some biology instructors from a neighboring school, to score the senior projects using the same criteria (see Anderson and Walvoord, 1991, for an example). These options create more work for the department, but they provide additional perspectives rather than relying only on the teacher's own criteria and evaluations of student performances.

Although this example was specifically oriented toward biology, this assessment process is applicable to all disciplines. The goal of direct evaluation is a reasonably valid and reliable assessment of student performance, evaluated by specific criteria. The results of this assessment would be aggregated in a format that will facilitate use of the data by its intended audiences. Often, the performances and the criteria can emerge from classroom work and contribute to the grading process as well as to departmental decision making and improvement in student learning.

Indirect Measures of Student Performance. Indirect measures offer evidence of student learning derived from sources other than direct observation of student performance—for example:

• Surveys of what or how well students or alumni think they learned (as distinguished from surveys of how well they liked the course or the instructor). A standardized student evaluation form that focuses heavily

on students' perception of their learning rather than merely on their satisfaction with the instructor is the IDEA survey from Kansas State University (http://www.idea.ksu.edu/).
- Surveys of employer satisfaction
- Career advancement, increased work satisfaction, and the like

Your own institution's office of institutional research or office of assessment may be conducting alumni surveys or gathering employment data. They may be able to add your questions to a survey they are already distributing or to break out data in ways that will be useful to your individual program.

If your research question is some version of determining whether your students are meeting your expectations, you now have methods to gather the data you need. You can identify one or more performances and evaluate students by your criteria, or you can gather indirect data about how well they learned. This information alone may serve your purposes, especially if the results show strong student performance and your purpose is to demonstrate that strong performance to others. However, many situations require that you seek to improve students' weaknesses. To do that, you must know why they are not performing as you had hoped. That requires addressing this question: What are the relations between the quality of student performance and other factors?

Establishing Relations Between Student Performance and Other Factors

Factors that correlate to quality of student performance could include student-related factors such as ethnicity, family income, motivation, or previous educational experience. Other factors could be related to the course itself, such as accelerated or traditional format, teaching methods, or use of technologies. It is important to make sure that you are actually measuring the factors you want to assess. Often the attempt to quantify the factors reveals complexities you had not considered. For example, a study that attempts to discover the relationship between students' academic performance and a new class Web page must explore how frequently students are using the Web page, for what purposes, and in what ways.

There are two common ways to establish relations between the quality of student performance measured and the other factors on which you collect data for assessing relations between student performance and other factors. The first way is through experimental design, using control and treatment groups. If you have two patches of the same kind of corn, planted in the same soil, and getting the same sun and rain, but you give fertilizer to the treatment patch and no fertilizer to the control patch, you have reason to believe that the fertilizer accounts for any differences. The difficulty, of course, is that in higher education settings, you cannot construct groups of students that are identical in all ways except one.

To deal with situations where they cannot control variables, researchers have developed various statistical methods to account for variables and indicate how much confidence can be placed on the connection between students' performance and a given factor, such as a particular teaching method or amount of time for face-to-face instruction. For example, the mathematics department at a large college with an accelerated program was using basically the same type of instruction for its accelerated sections (thirty-two contact hours) in Introductory Statistics as it was for its traditional sections (forty-five contact hours) of the same course. The mathematics department wanted to know whether students learned better under either the accelerated or traditional format. After conducting their research and statistically analyzing the relationship between each variable and learning, the department found that the strongest predictor of students' success in Introductory Statistics was not the type of course format (accelerated or tradition) but student scores on a math readiness test they all took. With that information, the department focused on a better system for directing low-scoring students into a college math workshop, providing tutoring, and helping instructors learn how best to deal with low-readiness students regardless of the instructional format being used.

Although control-treatment designs can be useful in higher education, they are often difficult, costly, or impossible. Another way of gathering evidence about relations is to ask students. For example, one of my colleagues, Madan Batra, employed a number of teaching methods for his international marketing course, including some that were quite time-consuming. He wanted to know which of his methods were most helpful to students and which might be eliminated or changed. He could not easily construct control and treatment groups, so he decided to rely on students' own perceptions of what was helpful to them. He constructed a questionnaire for his students in international marketing and administered it several times in subsequent terms. He asked students to rate how useful each of his teaching strategies was in helping them reach the various learning goals of the course (Batra, Walvoord, and Krishnan 1997). A few of the strategies received high marks from nearly all students. These key strategies, though time-consuming, he kept. A few strategies were rated minimally useful, so he could drop them. A few strategies got mixed reviews, so he asked his students to help him improve their usefulness. Useful guidance for researching the relationship between student performance and the use of various technologies can also be obtained through the Flashlight project of the Teaching Learning Technology Group (www.tltgroup.org).

Improving the Program on the Basis of Assessment Information

When individual faculty members undertake assessment, it is fairly straightforward for them to use the information they have gathered to make changes in curriculum or pedagogy. A more difficult issue is how departments and programs can use assessment information.

Table 4.1 presents a schema for planning departmental and program assessment. The schema shows the learning goals, the assessment methods chosen, and then how the information is used. Writing out such a schema can help clarify the purposes of assessment and prevent collection of data that will not be used. I suggest relying on usual department or program decision-making structures, such as committees and task forces, to make decisions based on assessment information. Ideally, assessment will become part of the department or program's way of life, informing all of its decisions wherever relevant.

Discovering Where Learning Is Being Assessed. Information such as standardized test results or alumni surveys that come directly to a program can be fed directly into the decision-making process. However, when the program relies on classroom work for assessment, it needs mechanisms to find out where in its curriculum various learning goals are being assessed and to get that information from the classroom to the program in a form useful for program decision making.

To discover where learning goals are already being assessed, the department or program can ask each instructor to fill in the relevant cells of a grid. For each of his or her courses, the faculty member indicates that she or he teaches to that goal at a high, middle, or low level and assesses it at a high, middle, or low level. In the example in Table 4.3, the instructor has indicated that in Biology 101, she teaches basic biological information at a high level (TH) and assesses it at a high level (AH). This means that a significant portion of the class time and exams are concerned with this goal. She teaches students to draw conclusions at a low level (TL) but does not assess that skill. In Biology 204, she teaches and assesses conclusion drawing at a high level. When every (or almost every) faculty member has filled out this grid for the classes that he or she teaches, a departmental committee can aggregate the data.

Collecting and Using Assessment Information for Decision Making. Once the program has identified where in its curriculum the relevant student knowledge and skills are being taught and evaluated, it can determine how to collect and use the assessments for program decision making. For example, one biology department defined as a goal for its majors that they should be able to use the scientific method for original research and to report that research orally and in writing to their peers (as shown in Table 4.1). The grid exercise showed that the faculty who taught the senior capstone course were already assessing those skills by assigning an original

Table 4.3.   Assessing Learning Goals in Biology

Learning Goal	Biology 101	Biology 102	Biology 204
Basic biological information	TH, AH		TH, AH
Draw conclusions from data	TL		TH, AH

Note: TH = teaching at a high level; TL = teaching at a low level; AH = assessing at a high level.

biological research project resulting in written and oral reports. There was no need to add another departmentwide test of students' ability to conduct and report scientific research when such classroom performance was in place.

One of the simplest, least time-consuming ways to get this information to a program is for teachers to use a primary trait scale or some similarly specific set of criteria to score student work. At an annual assessment meeting of the program, teachers present the aggregated results and their recommendations to their colleagues for their discussion and action. For example, a teacher might bring an example like Table 4.2 or the recommendation about graphing. When the teacher reports, the role of the program or department is threefold:

• To encourage and help the teacher. Perhaps she says, "The students were weak in area X, and I think I could improve their learning if I did such-and-such." Colleagues might say, "I think that will work," or "Have you thought of doing it this other way?" or "I'd be happy to look at some papers or visit your class to offer feedback if you wish."

• To use the information for program-level decision making. For example, in a business management department, faculty directing senior projects reported to the department that students were weak in their ability to define a good research question in the field. The department decided to make changes in two previous courses so that students would learn these skills earlier and practice them throughout the curriculum.

• The program records the results of their assessment meetings and reports as needed to other audiences such as accreditation or review boards. (A form for such reporting can be found in Walvoord and Anderson, 1998.)

To have teachers construct the criteria and evaluate student work is usually more efficient, because teachers often evaluate student work for the grading process. However, it is possible to have more program or departmental input, as the schema in Table 4.4 suggests.

The department might suggest guidelines for the teachers' criteria, or it might construct the criteria and measure student work against them. In one program, each faculty member gave a sample of work from his or her students' work to a departmental committee, which assessed it against departmental criteria. In another case, students were asked to collect a sample of their work in the major across time and present this portfolio to a faculty committee, which evaluated the portfolios against a set of departmentally designed criteria to determine what strengths and weaknesses show up in student work within the department. Each of these methods is more time-consuming than simply having the relevant faculty report his or her own scoring of student work to the department, but these alternatives provide broader perspectives than a single teacher's judgment.

Table 4.4.   Assessment Alternatives

Program Assessment Responsibilities	Teacher Alone	Department Committee	Outside Rater
Constructing the student performance			
Constructing the criteria			
Applying the criteria to the performance			

Helping Departments Change. Any method by which student classroom work is shared with a department or program requires that faculty feel secure and comfortable in sharing their students' work in the aggregate. The spirit of such a discussion must be facilitative and supportive rather than judgmental of the teacher. If students in the senior year are weaker than the program would like them to be, the entire program must take responsibility for trying to strengthen students' work.

Programs can implement an assessment plan, even when some of their members opt out or oppose the action. Assessment can start with part of the program's curriculum or faculty. For example, in one English department, the faculty who taught introductory courses got together to assess students' work at the end of the first year of study, even though the more senior faculty did not participate in that assessment. Effective assessment requires a certain level of healthy functioning and collegial spirit. If the program or department is seriously dysfunctional, that problem must be addressed before assessment can work.

It is important for a program to focus on those aspects of learning over which it has control and to choose the actions that seem most promising for real change. In accelerated programs, students' time pressures due to work and family responsibilities are likely to affect their learning (Wlodkowski, Mauldin, and Campbell, 2002), but the program cannot control these factors. Instead, it can work on factors it can influence, such as when courses are scheduled, enhancing student motivation, connecting with other faculty and peers, offering prompt and supportive advising, and helping students to learn to use their available time efficiently. Students themselves can be very helpful; the department might consider having student members on committees that conduct assessment or polling students to get their suggestions.

Departments also should plan change that is owned and supported by those who will implement those changes. For accelerated programs, this approach often means enlisting the support and expertise of adjunct as well as regular faculty. If changes in a particular course would seem helpful to students but an individual instructor is not willing to make them or does not attend meetings that address these changes, then the program has to deal realistically with the situation. It can bring the reluctant instructor on board or try other actions that might help students learn more effectively.

Conclusion

The goal of assessment for accelerated learning programs is nearly identical to traditional programs. Both formats have to address the three questions about student learning by providing reasonably valid and reliable information that is feasible to collect, given available knowledge and resources. With such information in hand, accelerated learning programs can improve their students' learning and report effectively to other audiences the outcomes of their work.

References

Anderson, V. J., and Walvoord, B. E. "Conducting and Reporting Original Scientific Research: Anderson's Biology Class." In B. E. Walvoord and L. P. McCarthy (eds.), *Thinking and Writing in College: A Naturalistic Study of Students in Four Disciplines.* Urbana, Ill.: National Council of Teachers of English, 1991.

Batra, M. M., Walvoord, B. E., and Krishnan, K. S. "Effective Pedagogy for Student Team Projects." *Journal of Marketing Education,* 1997, *19*(2), 26–42.

Walvoord, B. E., and Anderson, V. J. *Effective Grading: A Tool for Learning and Assessment.* San Francisco: Jossey-Bass, 1998.

Wlodkowski, R. J., Mauldin, J. E., and Campbell, S. "Early Exit: Understanding Adult Attrition in Accelerated and Traditional Postsecondary Programs." In *Synopsis: Higher Education Research Highlights.* Indianapolis: Lumina Foundation for Education, 2002.

BARBARA E. WALVOORD *is a fellow of the Institute for Educational Initiatives and concurrent professor of English at the University of Notre Dame, Notre Dame, Indiana.*

5

This chapter describes some of the essential criteria and elements for initiating and sustaining a successful accelerated degree program.

Developing and Maintaining Accelerated Degree Programs Within Traditional Institutions

William J. Husson, Tom Kennedy

Most traditional four-year colleges were designed to serve the population between eighteen and twenty-two years old. However, in the late 1970s, some colleges discovered the growing population of working older adult learners who wanted to return to college to complete undergraduate and graduate degree programs. To accommodate this population, these schools moved adult programs from being course focused to being degree focused. They also often created time-compressed courses and programs to accommodate adult learners who were familiar with corporate fast-track training programs. The combination of these two transformations was an instant success. Until these major innovations in higher education, adults who wished to complete degrees often faced up to eight years of evening classes and de facto second-class status. Continuing-education divisions for adult learners had to fight for classroom space and negotiate with daytime divisions to find sufficient faculty who would teach at night.

The growing field of adult learning, pioneered by Malcolm Knowles, Cyril Houle, and Patricia Cross, among others, began to strike a nerve with the corporate community. Corporations were seeking new ways to improve the knowledge of their workforce to create competitive advantages. When colleges met this need by creating accelerated degree programs, corporations supported adult students with tuition benefits, which acted as an incentive for them to return to college. Many older adults who had felt shut out from the traditional collegiate system responded to the opportunity. They now could complete upper-division course work and receive their degrees from an accredited institution in a fraction of the time that it would normally take on a traditional campus.

Most colleges offering accelerated degree programs provide courses in five- or eight-week formats, with students attending classes one night a week for a four-hour session. These twenty to thirty-two hours of contact sessions enable adults to accomplish their goals through a combination of intensive in-class sessions and out-of-class work. This approach significantly differs from the traditional forty- to forty-five contact hours per semester-long course with multiple class sessions per week.

Criteria for Successful Programs

Our perspective for selecting criteria to develop successful accelerated degree programs is based largely on the pragmatics of our own experience. Since 1982, one of us has managed accelerated undergraduate and graduate degree programs at a faith-based urban university, first as program director and then as academic dean for the past ten years. This program has grown to thirteen thousand students, with outreach throughout the United States. The other of us has been involved in adult college outreach programs at private colleges in Illinois and Colorado. He has coordinated a program providing accelerated learning consulting services to over thirty colleges and universities around the world.

We consider the following criteria critical to the success of these programs:

• *Learner-focused, market-sensitive approach.* At our institution, the phrase "learner focused, market driven" is our driving theme. We constantly strive to put the needs of our learners first, and academic programs reflect the needs of our community and employers, not the desires of faculty or administrators. Needs are determined through demographic studies, focus group meetings, competition analysis, and employer interviews.

• *Designed for adult learners.* For many years, adult students were subjected to a learning system basically designed for young people recently graduated from high school. We have come to know that adults have different learning needs than do postadolescent adults. The primary differences are older adults' motivation to learn and a wealth of life experiences that can be brought to bear on learning topics. While colleges seek to achieve the same learning outcomes for all their students regardless of age, it is imperative to design learning models specifically relevant to older adult learners. Adults need more interactive and participatory components with fewer lectures. They are also able to transfer their learning to application within a much shorter turnaround time when compared to traditional college-age students.

• *Passion for quality.* Because of their shorter time frame, accelerated degree programs are usually under intense scrutiny for academic quality;

college administrators and conventional faculty often hold them to a higher standard than they do traditional programs. Accelerated degree programs must show evidence of an appropriate level of rigor and degree of difficulty commensurate with the expectations of the academy for the subject matter covered. Standards and criteria must be set to determine whether program goals are being met and academic quality is maintained. This concern for quality means that reviews and evaluations should include student and alumni perceptions, objective assessment instruments, employer satisfaction surveys, and extensive outcomes research.

• *Program accessibility.* Over the years, many colleges have developed an intricate bureaucracy of regulations governing academic policies designed for the traditional student population. These policies often serve the purpose of maintaining a quality institution. However, in many instances, these regulations have created access barriers for nontraditional students. For example, many institutions will not recognize the validity of credit hours earned over five years ago at another institution. For some courses such as computer science, this regulation may be valid. However, in other courses, such as general math or composition, such a policy is unnecessarily regressive. The important things for colleges to take into consideration are the needs and nature of adult learners without compromising their academic integrity. The responsibility for the adult-friendly institutions is to accept appropriate credits previously earned, but indicate to the students where they do not fulfill current knowledge prerequisites for upper-division courses. In fact, a thorough review of existing academic policies is necessary when colleges wish to attract adult learners, especially colleges focused on accelerated undergraduate degree completion.

• *A variety of delivery options available at multiple sites.* Most colleges have provided limited options for their learners, with classes scheduled on campus during the daytime hours on weekdays. With the advent of adults returning to college, many institutions have creatively adapted their class schedules and provided a wide array of options to accommodate working adult learners. Classes for adults are now most often scheduled in the evenings and on the weekends, when they are better able to fit them into their busy schedules.

Organizations like the College Board (Brickell, 1992) have indicated that location is a primary decision factor for older adults returning to college, and as a result, many colleges have opened extension learning centers. These centers typically include spacious classrooms with tables and chairs in seminar style, breakout areas, computer lab facilities, and a range of personal reception services.

Colleges have also adapted alternative delivery methods for instruction. Most now make available guided independent study and Internet-based courses in addition to classroom delivery to serve the wide range of needs of their adult learner populations.

• *Excellent customer services.* The term *customer service* has not been often associated with colleges and universities. Customer service has been defined as "all the activities involved in making it easy for customers to reach the right parties within the company and receive quick and satisfactory service, answers, and resolution of problems" (Kotler, 2000). In fact, many colleges have ignored the need for quality services for their students, focusing instead on high-quality instruction. In serving adult students today, both high-quality instruction and superior customer services are required. When adult students' service needs are not being adequately met, they vote with their feet and migrate to better-served and better-supported institutions of learning. The goal of quality customer services is to serve the customer in a competent, efficient, convenient manner.

• *A commitment of leadership to foster the success and mission extension of these programs.* Some adult and continuing-education programs have been initiated at colleges and universities largely for the purpose of providing an additional source of revenue. However, the long-term viability of accelerated degree programs requires a sustained commitment on behalf of the senior leadership. If the purpose of offering programs for adult learners is not consistent with the institutional mission, the programs will fail or be eliminated when they become less productive. In some cases, the original institutional mission may not have been written in an inclusive manner and may have to be revised. As with other parts of the university, continuous investment in the infrastructure, learning support, and academic functions is necessary. However, in the case of accelerated degree programs, much of the investment required is dissimilar to the traditional system. Issues such as sufficient bandwidth for distant learners, computing capacity, and extension campus support services need to assume the same priority as dormitories, financial aid packaging for high school seniors, and traditional support services. Only strong leadership committed to the long-term success of all university programs can address these issues. The notion that one or another program is the heart of the university serves only to create an inappropriate caste system that is divisive and demoralizing.

Key Elements in Starting and Maintaining an Accelerated Degree Program

Although beginning an accelerated degree program may seem very challenging, the real gauntlet is sustaining a quality program after the first five years.

Institutional Purpose. Given the scope of the adult student market in the United States, many colleges may be tempted to offer accelerated degree programs that seriously strain their resources. For example, many schools have ventured into the computer science arena without appropriate funding or personnel to manage or maintain these programs. This is not to say that colleges cannot extend their reach when developing new programs for adult learners, but such efforts must be accompanied by sound planning. There is a need to consider the physical and human resource allocations commensurate to the task. Accelerated degree programs need proper resources if they are to succeed in the long term. These resources need to be spread across the infrastructure as well as the academic programs themselves. Just as a financial planner chooses a sufficiently distributed selection of stocks and bonds, colleges need to determine carefully what range of programs and disciplines will compose their accelerated offerings. Generally, business and social science programs are less resource intensive, especially compared to computer science, nursing, or engineering programs.

Programmatic Decision Processes. It is imperative for a business organization to review its strengths, weaknesses, opportunities, and threats carefully before undertaking any significant endeavor. When colleges look to begin or expand accelerated degree programs, this strategic analysis is imperative. The market for postsecondary education for older adults in the United States is extremely competitive and now includes a significant number of for-profit organizations and accredited corporate universities. Colleges must carefully determine where opportunity exists and how best to manage these opportunities.

Market surveys are an essential part of determining where appropriate niches may exist. Some colleges may be able to conduct these studies themselves, but most will rely on outside organizations to conduct the work. Generally, an outside organization will provide better and more objective data than internal sources will. The market study should include a comprehensive competitive analysis (review of all programs in a school's geographical area where potential students may be attracted to attend), surveys of employers, focus groups with potential students, sound demographic analysis (census data are most valuable), and level of employer tuition assistance. Even when an existing accelerated degree program looks to expand or change its extension sites, a number of these same strategies should be employed.

A number of organizations can provide geographical data so that a college can determine if the per capita income and college level of proposed target areas are consistent with either existing or desired populations. We have found in our work that most adults prefer to travel twenty minutes or less after work to a classroom location that is ideally situated between where they work and where they live.

Program Curricular Design. At the heart of the accelerated model is the centralized approach to curriculum development and management. In the typical traditional model, a faculty member is asked to offer a course in the college bulletin. The faculty member develops a syllabus, chooses texts and other learning support resources, prepares tests, and then offers the course from the materials she has prepared. The specific course is then identified with the faculty member who has prepared the course. In many respects, her version of the course belongs to her.

In the accelerated model, courses do not belong to individual faculty members. The college owns the courses in the same way as it owns the course description found in the bulletin. The college first determines which courses will comprise the program. Since there is a substantial investment in the development of each of the courses, the college may be more sensitive to the needs of adult students and the market in its choice of courses to offer compared to the traditional program. The college then contracts with individual faculty or teams of faculty to write the course syllabus. All of the faculty members who teach the course in the program then use this centralized version of the course syllabus.

Each course syllabus, or learning module as it is often referred to, has common elements: the bulletin description; appropriate learning outcomes; prerequisite knowledge requirements; goals and specific objectives; required learning resources, such as texts and readings; a guide for each class session with suggested activities; and student evaluation forms. The module, which defines the college's approach to each course, reflects the best judgment of the faculty who have participated in its development. The entire faculty will have ongoing opportunities to suggest changes and modifications for improvement.

Because the primary faculty in adult programs are adjunct faculty working in full-time professional positions, this centralized course syllabus is well suited for their use. This standard model offers consistency of purpose, process, and content across an array of different instructors. The oversight of the curriculum development is primarily in the hands of the academic administration of the program, while the facilitation of learning is primarily in the hands of the adjunct faculty. This modular design also allows for quality control in a number of ways. Each course has a designated syllabus design so that students can review the learning module prior to taking the course and be prepared. Each course identifies the texts and other learning materials that can be more efficiently managed and distributed to the learning sites or directly to the students by express delivery.

Working Professionals as Faculty. The faculty is the heart of any academic program. They should be chosen based on the needs of the learners, the curriculum, and their expertise in the subject matter. These judgments are based on their credentials, expertise of practice, experience in the workplace, and other considerations, including accreditation guidelines.

A number of the larger and more successful accelerated degree programs have developed a high-quality intake process for faculty, often referred to as the faculty assessment process. This process is an adaptation of a comprehensive approach to hiring managers developed by AT&T after World War II (Bray, 1998). In this process, prospective faculty are asked to participate in a variety of tasks and exercises that help determine the skills and abilities they can bring to the adult learner context. This process also determines faculty attitudes and skills to be effective mentors and instructors with adult students. Some faculty who work extremely well with traditional-age learners have great difficulty working with older adults. Conversely, some faculty who work well with adult learners have great difficulty working with younger students.

Most adult accelerated degree programs make extensive use of adjunct faculty. In fact, in most programs, the adjunct faculty form the primary teaching core. The working adult student looks to working professionals as faculty to provide the insights and know-how of the everyday professional community. Adjunct faculty must have the appropriate credentials for teaching—usually a master's or doctoral degree with prior course work in the areas they will be teaching. For the collegiate institution, there are financial benefits associated with adjunct faculty; they work part time, with reduced benefits and salary, which reduces the general labor costs associated with offering courses. Nevertheless, because their role is primarily teaching, the college will need to provide full-time faculty support in student advising and curriculum development.

Marketing Considerations. There is a world of difference between traditional college marketing and marketing accelerated degree programs for the adult student population. Older adults are looking for quality, value, access, and convenience (not necessarily in that order). They need to be reached through mass media rather than a network of high school counselors. In particular, adult admissions counselors use more of a direct sales approach and need to be skilled in techniques such as closing the sale. The focus of adult student counselors is convincing qualified adult student prospects that their program will meet more of their (prospects') needs than the competition will. To be able to do this competently, the counselor must be familiar with degree completion concepts, the particular degree programs at the institution, and the institution's transfer policies.

In our experience, the most successful accelerated degree programs have created a separate division for marketing their adult programs. This separation avoids dual functions existing in a single university office where one system will be dominant and the other will suffer because of the vast differences in form and style. An ideal accelerated degree marketing organization will include the following elements:

• A core of sales representatives (admissions counselors)
• A group of people managing the telephone or on-line inquiries (call center information and qualifying functions)
• An advertising and publications group
• A corporate outreach group, meeting regularly with large and medium-size businesses in the community

While the role of the sales representative is to counsel appropriate prospects into the program, someone needs to be funneling prospects to the sales group. Many persons fill this function, ranging from the receptionist to the call center operator. It is imperative that persons receiving calls from prospects be trained to qualify these individuals and then make recommendations for follow-up. Colleges are rightfully expected to direct those who do not qualify toward other educational opportunities at community colleges, vocational schools, or other postsecondary institutions. One recent trend among accelerated degree programs is to create call centers, where staff are trained in handling these calls and forwarding the qualified prospects to sales representatives. Another key to successful marketing is an effective sales representative, whose role is to match prospective students with programs that suit their expressed needs for continuing education.

Information Sessions. From what we see in the field, most successful programs offer information seminars to prospective students that are conducted by a sales representative. These seminars present an overview of the processes necessary to complete a degree at any institution and to suggest why the institution and its adult degree program will be the right choice for the participants. The advantage of the seminar approach is the supportive social climate. Older adults often feel uncomfortable in seeking information about returning to college. Their discomfort comes from a variety of sources. It could be that they were not successful in prior college experiences. They may feel that they should know more than they do about the process. They may be unsure as to what questions to ask or worry that they may be put in a situation that will be out of their control. When they see other adults at the seminar, they feel more comfortable about the process. They also can profit from others' questions and concerns. This group dynamic helps overcome fears and allows prospective adult students to visualize their participation in the college's programs.

The goal of the information seminar is to encourage prospective students who are eligible to apply to the program. Sales representatives can schedule individual appointments for students who cannot attend the seminar. However, these individual appointments can be time-consuming and do not have the impact of the group sessions. Most students, especially at the undergraduate level, will want to have some assurance of how their prior credits will transfer to the college. Some programs have prospective students meet with academic advisers to review their transcripts. However, we have found that the marketing process works best when the sales representatives have sufficient training to be able to guide students in approximating how their credit will transfer.

An official review of the transcripts will take weeks to months to complete due to the slow process of obtaining the appropriate transcripts. Although some adult students want to wait for an official review of their transcripts before they begin taking classes, most want to start as soon as possible. We have found it effective to allow undergraduate students to begin their studies as designated "special students" until their transcripts have been reviewed. The sales representative can continue working with the applicant until she has begun her first class. The sales representative, as the main link to the college, provides the needed trust and rapport with the applicant.

Promotional Materials and Advertising. Adult programs depend on the development of quality brochures and publications such as view books. These materials are similar to those published for traditional programs but focus on topics and photos attractive to adult students. These publications should be consistent with other university materials and look sophisticated enough to represent the quality of the program. How to determine how much material to send to students prior to their attendance at an information meeting or personal appointment is a difficult decision. Too much material can be prohibitive in cost; too little may discourage participation. A good idea is to review other institutions' materials in order to determine the local standard. Generally, graduate students require more detailed materials sent in advance to review than undergraduate students require. Graduate prospects generally take more time and compare more programs when making their decision.

Advertising is critical to the success of accelerated degree programs. Most programs advertise in newspapers, on radio and television, and in trade journals and publications. Traditional programs are unaccustomed to advertising in this fashion. Sometimes the faculty and other stakeholders find fault with the advertising style that may be needed to attract the adult population. Newspaper advertising costs have increased dramatically over the past decade and have become prohibitive in many regions of the country. Nevertheless, some newspaper advertising is necessary to position your institution among others advertising in the local papers.

Advertising may use several formats. Radio, especially rush-hour drive-time spots, has been a consistent winner in reaching adults. Radio ads need to be creative enough to get people's attention and sophisticated enough to maintain the quality image of the college. While television varies greatly from market to market, the costs for production and placement are usually prohibitive. A number of institutions use advertising companies that place advertising and use multiple customers' buying power to get the best placement at the most reasonable costs. These companies usually charge a percentage of the placement costs as their commission. Using a placement firm can relieve the marketing staff of a substantial amount of time and legwork.

A key area for recruitment is the corporate marketing connection. One of the reasons adult programs have become so popular is that businesses realize the value of an increasingly knowledgeable workforce. Most businesses have created tuition assistance programs to encourage their employees to continue their education. A successful strategy for adult degree programs is to have sales representatives call on corporate clients. This representative can establish contacts with local businesses, host brown bag lunches, place articles in company newsletters, and coordinate with company tuition reimbursement programs. These contacts engender corporate support through improved communication with these primary stakeholders.

Planning is always an essential ingredient for success in marketing. A well-designed market plan is essential to coordinate a quality program. The market plan should include basic assumptions about the size and scope of the programs planned, the identified niche, the characteristics of the customers, and the basic marketing and strategies. The plan should begin with a thorough review of the competition, including prices, market share, and engagement strategies.

Obstacles and Barriers to Accelerated Degree Programs

Accelerated programs have challenged the traditional thinking regarding the necessary time to complete college courses. Partly for this reason, these programs often come under intense scrutiny by various constituencies within more traditional colleges. Those working in accelerated programs may experience such skepticism as biased and unfair, especially when critics have little or no experience with adult learners and accelerated programs. This mistrust can be demoralizing to staff and faculty in accelerated programs when it comes from peers on the same campus.

The regional accreditation agencies, such as the North Central Association of Colleges and Schools, have focused on quality, primarily in terms of learning outcomes. They are asking colleges to demonstrate that predetermined learning outcomes are achieved in their courses and degree programs. This focus has enabled accelerated programs to demonstrate that there are multiple learning processes that can be used to achieve appropriate learning outcomes. Similar learning outcomes can be accomplished by different delivery systems (Wlodkowski and Westover, 1999).

For programs located in traditional institutions, it is important that intra-institutional communications be established. These apprehensions and cultural shifts can be addressed by inviting traditional faculty to review curriculum and participate in accelerated program activities. Unfamiliar academic delivery systems can be threatening to those responsible for the established order. In order to speak to these differences, critics should have an opportunity for dialogue and participation in program implementation. This is also a good time to make studies and other research on program quality available to them.

Conclusion

Accelerated degree programs for adult learners have grown enormously during the past twenty-five years. They have tapped the dramatic rise in the participation of older adult learners seeking higher education, now estimated to be over 40 percent of all college undergraduate students. These programs have combined innovative academic approaches with solid administrative techniques. Some of these are now part of for-profit institutions that serve only the adult population. Traditional colleges continue to attempt to serve adult learners, but many find they are seriously encumbered by their established framework and meet severe resistance from the traditional establishment. Nevertheless, we have constructed, as well as witnessed, successful accelerated degree programs within numerous traditional institutions that have the vision to see their mission as serving both adult and young adult populations and make the commitment to plan and carefully use their resources to do so. To this end, we have proposed the criteria for success and the elements necessary to make the vision of an effective accelerated degree program a reality.

References

Bray, D. M. *Centered on Assessment*. Charlotte, N.C.: Development Dimensions International, 1998.

Brickell, H. M. *Adults in the Classroom*. New York: College Entrance Examination Board, 1992.

Kotler, P. *Marketing Management*. Upper Saddle River, N.J.: Prentice Hall, 2000.

Wlodkowski, R. J., and Westover, T. "Accelerated Courses as a Learning Format for Adults." *Canadian Journal for the Study of Adult Education*, 1999, *13*(1), 1–20.

WILLIAM J. HUSSON *is vice president and academic dean of the School for Professional Studies at Regis University, Denver.*

TOM KENNEDY *is president of New Ventures of Regis University.*

The Service Oriented Field Experience presents adult distance learners with the experiential and reflective components of service-learning in an accelerated course. The result is often a transformative academic experience.

Distance Learning and Service-Learning in the Accelerated Format

Elise M. Burton

Internet-based distance education courses have transformed the landscape of higher education in the United States and internationally. The innovative and unprecedented ability to reach students directly by the virtual classroom has created exciting educational opportunities for working adult learners. The Service Oriented Field Experience (SOFE) (pronounced "Sophie") model is a hybrid of distance learning and service-learning that fuses the positive outcomes of both learning approaches in the context of an accelerated format. This model integrates the academic and technological skill sets that are so powerful in distance learning with experiential and contemplative outcomes that are not easily obtained in a virtual classroom (Alexander, Atkinson, Burton, and Mitchell, 2000).

The design of a SOFE course is premised on the belief that the learning outcomes of on-line accelerated courses, when well designed, well staffed, and institutionally supported, can be equal, if not superior, to those of traditional classroom-based models (Wlodkowski and Mauldin, 1999). The course is academically rigorous, as well as emotionally and spiritually challenging. By integrating a ten-day group service experience into an on-line format and presenting adult students with the challenges of direct service in an unfamiliar environment, the SOFE model encourages personal transformation among students.

The quotations from J. Shaw's student journal and N. Tembrock's newspaper articles are used with the permission of the authors.

The SOFE Model

SOFE is a three-credit master's-level course that is taught on-line over an eight-week period, with a ten-day service trip to Antigua, Guatemala, in the fifth week of the program. This is a challenging course designed for professionals in the education, nonprofit, health, social service, legal, and human rights fields or for individuals with interests in these areas. The student learns about the international nonprofit sector and prepares a final project that addresses the needs of a nonprofit organization based in Guatemala. Since 1999, three SOFE courses have been offered. These courses have been a collaborative effort between Regis University and La Asociación Nuestros Ahijados, a Guatemalan-based charity.

SOFE courses require the support of two on-line facilitators, one based in the United States (and referred to as the stateside facilitator) and the other in Guatemala (the onsite facilitator), to coordinate the distance and service components of the class.

The SOFE model has three essential components: Phase I: Distance Learning Component; Phase II: Service Learning Component; and Phase III: Closure and Final Project Completion. The stateside facilitator and the onsite facilitator work together throughout the class, although the stateside facilitator is primarily responsible for the on-line and administrative components of Phase I. The onsite facilitator focuses on the experiential and service aspects of Phase II. Both facilitators address closure issues and grade final project submissions during Phase III.

In addition to a detailed course syllabus, students are provided with a manual that includes an overall course description, liability waivers and medical disclosure forms, information regarding personal safety, a section on calculating costs, a packing list, a detailed in-country schedule, general information regarding the SOFE experience, and a form that they submit to verify that they have read the manual (Atkinson, 1999).

Phase I: Distance Component. During the first four weeks, SOFE is much like any other on-line accelerated course, with the important exception that students know that in a few weeks, they will be living, learning, and providing a service together in a very different environment. All academic discussions are conducted in an asynchronous threaded discussion forum. On-line audio and visual assignments are frequently provided to supplement assigned texts. The first weeks of class present students with an overview of the international nonprofit sector and the recent social and economic history of Guatemala. Students are encouraged to analyze the information provided and to formulate their own understanding of the causes of Guatemalan social conflict and socioeconomic inequities.

During these first four weeks, the stateside facilitator is responsible for addressing the basics of the on-line course: ensuring that the class Web page is on-line and available, fostering a closely knit on-line class environment, and monitoring and responding to threaded discussions. In addition, the stateside facilitator ensures that all pretrip administrative and travel matters are attended to, including medical disclosures and waivers of liability. Meanwhile, the onsite facilitator focuses on matching students individually or in small groups with nonprofit organizations in and around Antigua for their service project. Students are variously assigned (individually or in teams) to specific projects identified by the onsite facilitator as being useful to a Guatemalan nonprofit organization and of interest to the student. The overriding goal is for each student project to provide a useful service to an organization that does not otherwise have the resources to address the issue undertaken.

The nature of student projects is determined largely by the experiences and interests that each adult student brings to the class. These service projects might include program evaluations, marketing projects, in-depth studies regarding program implementation, cross-border legal issues, or financial reviews. Such projects create the opportunity for students to understand and address on a microscale the practical problems that small, nonprofit organizations outside the United States face every day. They also provide opportunities to formulate theoretical and practical methods for recognizing and solving these problems. Throughout the course, students reflect on the concepts of service, commitment, and vocation in their own lives and the lives of others. In addition, by working with and learning from groups that work directly with the poor of Guatemala, students are exposed to a more realistic understanding of what can be accomplished by national and international service organizations (Alexander, Atkinson, Burton, and Mitchell, 2000).

During Phase I, the opportunity to participate for an hour in a real-time chat is offered in each of the first four weeks of the class. These chats are primarily social in nature, in that all academic matters are addressed using asynchronous threads. The days and times that these chats are held is varied to accommodate the students' work and family schedules. Transcripts of these chats are provided to those who cannot or choose not to attend. Chatroom topics are student directed, and many of the matters discussed are covered in the detailed planning manual already provided to them (Atkinson, 1999). Nevertheless, because students know that they will all soon meet and work together, and some are understandably anxious about their impending travel experience, these optional chats are very popular. Questions and discussions in the chatroom often include what to wear, what to bring as gifts or donations, what travel insurance to purchase, and safety concerns.

According to conventional wisdom, in many on-line courses, both students and facilitators find "real-time" chats to be frustrating and unproductive. In a SOFE course, students find the real-time virtual classroom environment a useful tool to get to know those with whom they will be sharing an intense ten-day period during Phase II. An interesting example of this revolves around donations. Students are encouraged to bring only one carry-on bag for their personal use and to use their checked baggage for donations for the poor. A unique dynamic occurs in the chatroom as students share their ideas for filling these donation bags. One student may describe receiving as many as three hundred toothbrushes donated by her dentist; another may report receiving church donations (literally a portion of Sunday's collection plate) toward the purchase of over-the-counter medicines. Still another student may recount her success (or frustration) when canvassing her neighborhood for used clothing. As such ideas are exchanged and duplicated across the country, student anticipation for the trip rises.

Phase II: Service-Learning Component. Around the fifth week of the class, SOFE students travel across the United States to participate in their ten-day service-learning trip to Guatemala. Most of the students are able to meet at an airport hub and travel together. When they arrive at the airport, their excitement is palpable as they meet face-to-face for the first time. The on-line bonding that has previously occurred is manifested in the greetings and hugs that students exchange. The plane ride is a bustle of questions and shared information as students work through an engaging assignment during the final five hours of the trip.

Arriving in Guatemala. The group is met at the Guatemala City Airport by members of La Asociación Nuestros Ahijados with a van for the students and a pickup truck for their donations. Under the guidance of the onsite facilitator, these employees and volunteers of the Antigua-based charity have worked hard in preparation of supporting the learning experience of Phase II. The drive to Antigua takes about two hours. There, students stay at family-owned bed and breakfasts located near the La Asociación Nuestros Ahijados's community development center, which is known as the Dreamer Center (El Centro Soñador). Accommodations are comfortable but not luxurious, and most meals are provided. Students who do not speak Spanish are paired with those who have some command of the language.

Students have been forewarned that barking dogs, roosters that decide that 2:00 A.M. is a good time to start the day, and tourists returning late from a boisterous evening may interrupt their night's rest. They have also been told that they will see and may directly experience those disturbing things that are associated with violence and poverty. Despite these expectations and inconveniences, most students greet their first full day in Antigua with enthusiasm.

The First Day. Prior to their arrival, the onsite facilitator has provided students with a detailed plan for each day of the trip. This planning manual includes the following caveat: "Delays and changes are inevitable in every facet of daily life in Guatemala. Recognizing this, Guatemalans are often amused by foreigners who get stressed out by breakdowns, long lines, and glitches in organized events. 'Go with the flow' is the best way to get into the rhythm of life in Guatemala" (Atkinson, 1999, p. 22). After breakfast with their host families, students gather at the Dreamer Center to review the itinerary for the trip. Great emphasis is placed on personal safety and staying together. Although free time to journal and enjoy the sights of Antigua is scheduled, staff emphasize to the students that this experience is not designed to be a vacation.

Student Experiences. In addition to the formal service project, the onsite facilitator and his staff have planned authentic learning opportunities for the SOFE students during their stay. These experiences include talking with former street children, serving lunch and playing soccer with inmates at a local prison, hearing the stories of those who have survived massacres, meeting with human rights activists, and working with the poor to construct one-room houses in slums so fetid that tapeworms can live in the soil as they might in an intestinal tract. An example of the nature of these experiences is documented in the following excerpt from an article written by a SOFE student on her return from Guatemala:

> Our group traveled to the Indian village of Chipiacul, Chimaltenango, where in 1982, an army massacre took place. We listened to Sonia tell her story of family members being tortured and murdered, and how she survived because she was rescued as a child by Patrick Atkinson, the founder of The God's Child Project. Then we listened to a group of older women, still living in the village, who told individual accounts of their husbands', sons', and fathers' torture and death. The stories were horrid nightmares, sickening examples of dehumanization and blatant ethnic cleansing. As they spoke in sobbing phrases, it seemed that the unfathomable massacre occurred just last week rather than 18 years ago. We sobbed with them. I was struck by how appreciative the women were of our listening, our sharing of their burden and our acknowledgement of the horrible acts that happened. This amazed me. Fear, anger, and trauma have silenced them for so many years [Tembrock, 2000, p. 4].

The Service Project. During their trip to Antigua, students work and study directly with an organization to which they have been assigned for purposes of their final project. This may take them out of Antigua to mountain communities where poverty is also deeply rooted. These activities allow them to better understand the context of the organization they are seeking to serve and to produce a final project on their return to the United States that is useful to that organization.

The final projects envisioned and planned for by the students often change when they are confronted by the frequently grim reality that the organizations they intend to serve face. An example of how final projects change as a direct result of the service trip occurred in the March 2001 SOFE class. Some students were assigned the task of assisting a group called La Asociación Femenina Para El Desarrollo Rural (AFEDER; Women's Association for Rural Development), located in the mountain hamlet of Sacala. Two students were assigned the task of providing the group of approximately twenty-five weavers with a strategic plan for marketing their goods. Elaborate ideas such as creating a Web page for the sale of goods over the Internet and connecting these women with vendors in parts of Guatemala with large tourist populations had been researched and discussed with great anticipation during the Internet portion of the class and prior to their two-day visit to Sacala. Two other students were assigned to review the overall health and medical conditions of the same hamlet. When they arrived in this remote community, it became apparent that electricity was intermittent, and most of the community was illiterate and unprepared to work with a computer even if one were available. Furthermore, the village had no running water.

The absence of potable water had immediate, obvious, and severe implications for the health and well-being of all members of the community. In an example of how adult learners can apply their life skills and enhance their own learning experiences, these four students joined to alter their final project plans radically. Those assigned to the creation of a strategic business plan refocused their objectives and partnered with the other two students to raise funds to drill a well in Sacala. They pooled their resources, purchased weavings from the AFEDER cooperative, and planned to hold a silent auction to sell the weavings when they returned to the United States. Their final project included their strategic plan for this endeavor. The two thousand dollars they raised at a university auction gained matching funds from the Rigoberta Menchu foundation in Guatemala. A well providing fresh water to the people of Sacala should be completed soon with these funds.

Closure. An important facet of Phase II involves closure for the students prior to leaving Guatemala. Students are often unprepared to return to their comparatively comfortable lives in the United States after being exposed to so much poverty in such a short period of time. In order to diffuse the sense of displacement and slight depression that students invariably feel on their return home, the final day in Antigua is one of recollection and remembrance. The intent is to instill within the students a sense of the gift they have received: to be able to share what they have learned with their own communities when they return home. In order to begin to accomplish this purpose, there is a half-day of silent reflection near the end of the students' time in Guatemala. During this reflection, they share breakfast, spend two hours in contemplation and journaling, followed by a silent lunch. This activity closes with a native mass celebrated with local children. The second part of this closure process takes place on-line during the third and final phase of the course.

Phase III: Completion of Final Projects and Closure. The final stage of the SOFE class involves a follow-up over the Internet and the completion of final projects for submission to one another and the intended organization. Students and facilitators continue closure discussions and reflect together on-line as to how final projects should be completed. In many instances, the nature of final projects has changed after each student has had an opportunity to interact directly with the organization for which he or she is preparing the project. A frequent influence on this student revision is the realization that the extreme poverty of the people they worked with and care about is far greater than they initially imagined. The following journal remarks are representative of this transformation:

November 23—Back to the U.S.

Returning to the land of 20-pound Thanksgiving turkeys and market values was a rude awakening after spending 10 intense days in a world of suffering, spirituality, and authentic struggle. I learned a tremendous amount through the rare, first-hand experiences, which allowed me to see, hear, smell, feel, and somehow understand suffering. I feel angered by the oppression and violence the Mayan people have been and continue to be subjected to. And while there is much despair, I recognized an unquenchable spirit of courage, tenacity, and resiliency in the people's existence. This gives me hope. I feel a heightened sense of my own human rights and opportunity, and I am encouraged to work for equality, peace, and justice [Tembrock, 2000, p. 4].

Achieving a Meaningful Hybrid

Even universities that are open to innovative approaches to education, such as accelerated and distance programs, are sometimes wary of change. At Regis University the chair of the Department of Nonprofit Management, an essential advocate of this course at an institutional level, played a third and crucial role in creating the successful SOFE courses.

The Stateside facilitator needs to be an effective on-line facilitator and, in the context of a Guatemalan SOFE experience, culturally competent as well as competent in Spanish. However, the largest responsibility for creating a safe and meaningful SOFE experience falls on the onsite facilitator and his staff during Phase II. The onsite facilitator provides students with meaningful service projects and experiences that are beyond what a casual visitor to Guatemala would encounter. In the course used as an example in this chapter, the onsite facilitator had eighteen years of work experience in Guatemala and ten years as the executive director of La Asociación Nuestros Ahijados, which serves the needs of over twenty-five hundred poor children and their families.

For a safe SOFE experience, obtaining legal waivers of liability and medical disclosures prior to departure from the United States is essential. Direct and detailed language is provided in the planning manual (Atkinson, 1999). Nevertheless, some students, especially adults who guard their privacy, need to be urged to disclose all medical conditions and are strongly assured of their privacy. During the first SOFE class, one student neglected to mention a medical condition that, for personal reasons, the student was not comfortable sharing. Although no emergency arose, it could have, and time lost by not having the details of this condition in the student's medical disclosure could have been critical. As a consequence, great emphasis has been placed in subsequent SOFE courses that notarized medical disclosure forms are reviewed only for completeness and signature and then placed in a sealed envelope, to be accessed only in the event of a medical emergency. Students are advised to make certain that everything they would want a doctor to know in the event of an accident is included.

Despite the emotionally challenging aspects of the class, most adult students tend to be admirable in their behavior and accepting of the individual quirks of others throughout Phase II. With both the stateside and onsite facilitators readily available, small disagreements are usually diffused. Another challenging aspect of a SOFE course however, is that no matter how graphic the readings and discussions during Phase I are, there is sometimes a student who arrives in Antigua expecting something akin to a packaged tour. In one instance, a student who shared with colleagues that he planned to escape from group activities at the first opportunity and relax was overwhelmed when confronted with the poverty of the area. This student was given a few days away from the group and ultimately chose to withdraw from the class. As a consequence, in subsequent SOFE courses, the emotionally challenging aspects of the experience are consistently underscored and discussed.

Cost concerns are an issue that challenges the SOFE model. Students need to pay for their tuition, airfare, airport tax, in-country expenses (approximately $600), books, vaccines, and in some cases the fees associated with obtaining a passport. All this, when combined with the need to take ten days off work, does preclude students who would otherwise participate. Some financial subsidies and scholarships have been made available to students, but the challenge remains that some students cannot afford to take a SOFE class.

New SOFE Courses

Thus far, the SOFE model has been implemented only in collaboration with La Asociación Nuestros Ahijados in Guatemala. However, presuming that an onsite facilitator and staff are available at the service site, the Phase II service portion of the SOFE model could occur almost anywhere in order to achieve its objectives of unifying adult on-line students in a specific environment of service. To date, SOFE courses have focused on issues of nonprofit management at the master's level. However, this model could also be used in the context of many different accelerated distance programs, both graduate and undergraduate. In our experience, in addition to meeting and surpassing course learning outcomes, students have formed lasting alliances and strong friendships.

Currently, student and institutional enthusiasm for SOFE experiences outside Guatemala have stimulated the initiation of three courses based on the SOFE model, currently in the planning stages, for a Navaho reservation in the United States and a community in Ghana. A SOFE course in South Africa has just been successfully completed.

Conclusion

The service component of a SOFE course complements the typical design of an accelerated distance course by providing adult students the opportunity to work together to address real-world issues as they learn. As a hybrid of distance learning and service-learning, the SOFE model gives adult students learning opportunities generally unavailable to them in a typical accelerated course. In our experience, students have formed strong and lasting relationships that have been forged through the travel and service aspects of this course.

The greatest benefit of the SOFE experience is its transformative nature. Adult distance students who serve and learn together change their worldviews. Consequently, SOFE courses are particularly significant for adult distance learners who, while well equipped to respond to and meet the actual needs of others in the learning context, are not often given the opportunity to apply these skills to real situations.

In the words of one former SOFE participant, "It's extraordinary that sometimes you have to journey to a place totally outside your normal environment to discover the parts of yourself that help you recognize what can be done in your own backyard" (Shaw, 2001).

References

Alexander, P., Atkinson, P., Burton, E., and Mitchell, S. "Service-Oriented Field Experience: A Fusion of Distance and Service Learning in Accelerated Programs." Panel presentation to the Association for Research on Nonprofit Organizations and Voluntary Action, New Orleans, La., Nov. 2000.

Atkinson, P. "Planning Manual for an International 'Service-Oriented Field Experience' to Guatemala, Central America." Denver: Department of Nonprofit Management, School for Professional Studies, Regis University, 1999.

Shaw, J. R. SOFE, Student Journal. Mar. 2001.

Tembrock, N. "Searching for Justice in Central America." *Paonia* (Colorado) *Valley Chronicle,* Jan. 2000. [http://www.godshild.org/newsarticles/valley_chronicle.htm].

Wlodkowski, R. J., and Mauldin, J. E., "Report on Accelerated Learning Research Project Phase 3." Denver: Regis University School for Professional Studies and New Ventures, Dec. 30, 1999.

Additional Resources

La Asociación Nuestros Ahijados Webpage: <http://www.ana.org.gt>
The GOD'S CHILD Project Webpage: <http://www.GodsChild.org>

ELISE M. BURTON is associated with Higher Education Executive Associates in Colorado and is an affiliate faculty member of Regis University's School for Professional Studies, Department of Nonprofit Management. She designed and implemented the first SOFE course with Paul Alexander and Patrick Atkinson.

This chapter situates accelerated learning programs, and in particular cohort-based programs, within a critical analysis using concepts from Herbert Marcuse and Erich Fromm.

A Critical Theory Perspective on Accelerated Learning

Stephen D. Brookfield

As those working within accelerated learning programs know all too well, conventional educational wisdom holds that such programs invariably suffer from the reduced contact time that is their defining feature. A reduction in class hours is the very reason that such programs are called accelerated. Critics of the accelerated model assume that the more time that learners and teachers have for face-to-face meetings, the more likely it is that trust will develop among those involved. Only with time can learners judge whether teachers' words and actions are consistent and whether teachers can be relied on to behave fairly, openly, and honestly. Moreover, the argument goes, increased contact time is necessary for learners to develop intellectual rigor and analytical depth. Teachers are said to need sufficient time to model the analytical behaviors they wish to encourage in learners. Extended contact time and a teacher's skilled help are also believed to be necessary so that learners are able to uncover dimensions and applications of ideas that would remain hidden in on-line or independent study environments. Finally, the interpersonal ease encouraged by time spent in class is thought by some to enable the development of peer learning in a way that would be problematic within accelerated formats.

This conventional wisdom comes dangerously close to the "four legs good—two legs bad" logic of Orwell's *Animal Farm*. Increased contact time is seen as an unalloyed good and the reduced contact time of accelerated learning formats as an irretrievable deficit that calls into question the fundamental validity of this form of education. I believe this position to be vastly oversimplified and, in some instances, plain wrong. There is nothing inherently ennobling or enriching about a group of adults spending a

NEW DIRECTIONS FOR ADULT AND CONTINUING EDUCATION, no. 97, Spring 2003   © Wiley Periodicals, Inc.

greater, rather than smaller, amount of time in a teacher's presence. If an adult learning environment is characterized by incompetence, duplicity, narrow-mindedness, confusion, or an abuse of power, extending the amount of time learners spend in this environment does nothing in and of itself to address or change these factors.

The corrupting influence of extensive contact time is a theme implicit in the work of critical theorists Herbert Marcuse and Erich Fromm. According to Marcuse, the more time learners spend in group learning contexts, the more difficult it becomes for them to achieve the detachment from everyday experience necessary to the development of a truly critical perspective. Time spent with peers and teachers often impedes what he called rebellious subjectivity. In Fromm's view, group learning carries with it the danger of automaton conformity, of the learner's following the crowd because to stand against dominant opinion is to risk being regarded as antisocial, uncooperative, not a good sport. With increased time together comes the increased possibility that tyranny of the majority will act to diminish the power and presence of minority, dissenting voices.

In this chapter, I take the concepts of rebellious subjectivity and automaton conformity and apply them to the debate concerning the inherent implausibility of accelerated learning and to an analysis of some tendencies evident within cohort-based accelerated learning programs. Such programs exhibit features that offer opportunities for the development of critical consciousness—particularly for what Marcuse called rebellious subjectivity—that are absent from traditional programs. However, it is also true that such programs (particularly those that entail a degree of student negotiation of the curriculum) run the risk of falling foul of the influence of Fromm's automaton conformity.

Accelerated Learning and the Possibility of Rebellious Subjectivity

The critical theory tradition tends to favor collectivities of learners and to argue for Freirean-style culture circles in which people problematize common experiences and learn from each other. Accelerated learning formats, because they are often linked to proprietary institutions, are seen in the critical tradition as suspect. There is a belief that such programs represent a commodification of learning in which businesses sell a product (a degree) in a marketplace in a way designed to undercut the competition. A competitive edge is gained by asking students to spend less time studying and less time in the presence of a teacher or other learners than would be required in a conventional degree program. Traditionally inclined academics who value content knowledge and view the teacher as repository and transmitter of such knowledge are particularly scathing about the lack of intellectual rigor they perceive in accelerated learning. Cutting down the time students spend with teachers is seen as an unpardonable sin, robbing learners of the chance to develop analytical skills of a high order or preventing them from gaining a full appreciation of the complexities of a subject.

The deep suspicion of individualism within critical theory—of people thinking and acting as if they were independent entities, free of history, with no obligation to the common good—also works against accelerated learning's emphasis on the individual's moving through a program at the most rapid pace possible. To many in the critical tradition, individualism is condemned as an ideology that is part of the capitalist superstructure, one that emphasizes capitalist values of competitiveness, separation, and the efficient division of labor over solidarity and collaboration. An emphasis on individualism is often taken as a sign of political naiveté, an indication that the writer concerned has swallowed the "pulling yourself up by the bootstraps/ anyone can be president" ideology of individual betterment. Indeed, encouraging people to think that "there is no such thing as society" (in Margaret Thatcher's infamous phrase) is often viewed by critical theorists as an effective way for the dominant culture to prevent the development of class, racial, ethnic, or gender solidarity.

The late Herbert Marcuse offered a different perspective within the critical theory tradition. Like other Frankfurt school theorists familiar to adult educators (particularly Fromm, Horkheimer, and Adorno), Marcuse condemned the commodification of life. His work described the "comfortable, smooth, reasonable, democratic unfreedom" (Marcuse, 1964, p. 1) of the affluent society in which the acquisition of goods became the purpose of life. For Marcuse, however, escape from such a society was not just a matter of collective action. It also entailed rebellious subjectivity— a deeply personal change in the instincts and impulses of each individual's psyche. Such a change was dependent on characteristics such as inwardness, privacy, distance, and isolation that are not strongly emphasized in critical adult education but that are common currency among accelerated on-line programs that value learners' pacing themselves in their studies. Only with isolation, distance, and separation could a learner develop rebellious subjectivity.

For Marcuse, a period of separation from cultural and social influences was vital for people to develop independent critical thought. When we spend the majority of our lives engaged in social living in an administered society, we experience only dominated living. In the pressure to conform to common expectations, the chance for individual thought is lost. The only way people can come to a truly critical perspective is by distancing themselves in some manner from the stupefying influence of commonsense ways of thinking, feeling, and speaking. Hence, in Marcuse's view, isolation and separation, the conditions of true autonomy, are potentially revolutionary, the precursors to a commitment to social change. As such, educational formats such as accelerated learning programs that involve substantial amounts of independent study, self-directed learning, or on-line education and that emphasize periods of learner isolation and separation from institutional services and peer interaction, could actually be considered to offer more, not fewer, opportunities for the development of critical awareness.

From this perspective, the individualistic emphasis evident in some self-paced, accelerated learning programs now becomes a possible opening for the development of a different kind of consciousness. Some of the most common themes within the accelerated learning discourse are those of autonomous thinking and self-directed learning. The explosion of self-paced on-line learning that has occurred over the past decade is often claimed to represent an important increase in the adult learner's autonomous exercise of control over how and when she learns. If a learner chooses to pace herself in an accelerated manner, this is often believed to represent a valuable form of student-centered adult education. However, the political dimensions to self-direction, and by implication to autonomy, have largely been ignored. To Marcuse, autonomous thought was a necessary condition for the development of any kind of social movement intended to resist domination. But because of technological domination and the consumerist manipulation of needs, "independence of thought, autonomy and the right to political opposition are being deprived of their basic critical function" (1964, p. 1). The stifling influence of dominant ideology could be reversed or challenged only by the development of independent thought; "intellectual freedom would mean the restoration of individual thought now absorbed by mass communication and indoctrination" (p. 4).

In an era of total domination, how could true autonomy be realized? Marcuse turned to the liberating power of art, an avenue for social change well known to cultural workers in popular education through the theater of the oppressed, street art, community murals and video, independent film, rock and roll, and punk, folk, and rap music. But it was not this kind of overtly political "people's art" that interested Marcuse. To him, true autonomy, that is, separation from the contaminating influences of conformity and consumerism, arose out of the individual's opportunity to abstract herself from the day-to-day reality of the surrounding culture. For an altered consciousness to develop, it was necessary for the adult to experience a fundamental estrangement from commonly accepted ways of thinking and feeling. Immersion in artistic experience was one way to induce this estrangement. Contact with certain artistic forms offered a pathway of separation, a way of breaking with the rhythms of normal life. This focus on inwardness, on subjectivity, as liberating is very much at odds with how contemporary educational activists think of the political function of art. Privacy, isolation, and inwardness have become suspicious ideas, indicating an irresponsible withdrawal from political commitment. Indeed, a common criticism of accelerated learning is that its intensive pace fosters the individual determination to complete a course of study as quickly as possible without regard to the learning group's welfare. How, then, could Marcuse regard separateness as liberating?

The answer lies in Marcuse's belief that ideological domination is so complete that it suffuses all interpersonal communications. Collaborative artistic work, team productions, and other forms of group activity often found in educational programs with high amounts of contact time are all automatically directed toward making systems work better, rather than with challenging the moral basis of those systems. Each person's belief in the basic efficacy regarding the way society is organized is reinforced by contact with others in the society. Removing ourselves from the influence of others is a revolutionary act, a step into, rather than a retreat from, the real world. From this perspective, accelerated learning programs that emphasize self-paced learning, individualized programs of study, or on-line instruction are raising the chances that learners will experience the degree of separation from the mainstream body of learners necessary for the development of rebellious subjectivity.

Memory is crucial to rebellious subjectivity as a temporary break with reality: "Remembrance is a mode of dissociation from the given facts, a mode of 'mediation' which breaks, for short moments, the omnipresent power of the given facts. Memory recalls the terror and the hope that passed" (Marcuse, 1964, p. 98). Memory is a route out of the usual way of experiencing everyday life and hence a source of the estrangement Marcuse felt was crucial to developing revolutionary consciousness. In his view, the distance from daily existence that memory sometimes provides is key to the development of all forms of independent, critical thought. The further we get from the quotidian, the better chance we have of breaking out of domination. As a general rule, "it is the sphere farthest removed from the concreteness of society which may show most clearly the extent of the conquest of thought by society" (Marcuse, 1964, p. 104).

When we live our lives in association with others, it becomes difficult to establish the necessary distance for autonomous thought. In all areas of our lives, we are subject to "aggressive and exploitative socialization" (Marcuse, 1978, p. 5) that forces us into constant association with those who believe things are working just fine. For example, the contemporary emphasis on collaboration and teamwork, such a venerated practice in adult education, has "invaded the inner space of privacy and practically eliminated the possibility of that isolation in which the individual, thrown back on himself alone, can think and question and find" (Marcuse, 1964, p. 244). To Marcuse (1964), privacy was "the sole condition that, on the basis of satisfied vital needs, can give meaning to freedom and independence of thought" (p. 244). It was therefore no accident that for most people, privacy "has long since become the most expensive commodity, available only to the very rich" (p. 244).

Marcuse's lamentation of the passing of privacy and his stress on the revolutionary power of detachment and isolation sit uneasily alongside the belief of many adult educators that learning (particularly critical learning) is inherently social. Introspective analysis of a private and isolated sort is thought to lead us into perceptual dead-ends. To me, critical reflection is a social learning process in which we depend on others to be critical mirrors reflecting back to us aspects of our assumptive clusters that we are unable to see. I have, like many others, urged that true adult education is collaborative and collective, the building of a learning community in which the roles of teachers and learners are blurred. In my own practice within accelerated learning cohort programs, I have emphasized collaborative work as the norm, even to the extent of discouraging individually written doctoral dissertations. I have felt that this co-creation of knowledge mirrored best practices in the field, as seen in Freirean culture circles, the Highlander folk school, social movements, and participatory research. To me, isolation has usually been seen as a step backward, a retreat into the divisive, competitive, privatized creation of knowledge characteristic of capitalism. How on earth can privacy and isolation challenge the social order?

To Marcuse, this question is asinine. In his view, we should be asking instead, "How can we possibly challenge the social order *without* experiencing first the separation that isolation provides?" A person who experiences a deeply personal, completely private reaction to a work of art "steps out of the network of exchange relationships and exchange values, withdraws from the reality of bourgeois society, and enters another dimension of existence" (Marcuse, 1978, p. 4). This is the dimension of inwardness, of liberating subjectivity. Such subjectivity is liberating because we are moved by primal aesthetic and creative impulses, not the dictates of majority opinion or commonsense criteria of beauty. Privacy, inwardness, and isolation are all revolutionary because they play the role of "shifting the locus of the individual's realization from the domain of the performance principle and the profit motive to that of the inner resources of the human being: passion, imagination, conscience" (p. 5).

According to this logic, a truly critical adult education would be concerned not just with locating itself within existing social movements. It would also be seeking to create opportunities for people to experience the privacy and isolation they need for memory, introspection, and meditation to trigger a rupture with present-day experience. This rupture is not just a sort of spiritual awakening, but an experiential dissonance that will jerk people into an awareness of how life could be different. Only with distance and privacy can a new sensibility develop that "would repel the instrumentalist rationality of capitalism" (Marcuse, 1972, p. 64). Here we see the multiple possibilities, and the contradictions, for accelerated learning programs as sites for critical practice. On the one hand, accelerated learning could certainly be cited as an example of the instrumental rationality of capitalism; after all, the concern is often to move as many people (paying customers) through a program as quickly as possible, so that more may be recruited into the next cycle. On the other hand, accelerated learning programs that break with the need for groups of students to meet face to face on a weekly basis do pry open a fissure for individual detachment in the wall of groupness that surrounds traditional adult education.

Automaton Conformity

Automaton conformity was the term used by Erich Fromm (like Marcuse, a German who fled Nazi Germany and settled in the United States) to describe the process of social manipulation that results in the adult striving to be exactly the same as he or she imagines the majority to be. The flight into automaton conformity was one of the two possible responses Fromm identified to the fear of freedom. The central thesis of *Escape from Freedom* (1941) is that "the process of growing human freedom . . . means growing isolation, insecurity, and thereby growing doubt concerning one's own role in the universe, the meaning of one's life, and with all that a growing feeling of one's own powerlessness and insignificance as an individual" (p. 51). The individual attempts to escape this burden of freedom "by transforming himself into a small cog in the machine, well fed, and well clothed . . . yet not a free man but an automaton" (p. xii). In this way, people escape the anxiety produced by the awareness of their freedom: "If I am like everybody else, if I have no feelings or thoughts which make me different . . . I am saved; saved from the frightening experience of aloneness" (Fromm, 1956, p. 13).

One of Fromm's critiques of American higher education was that it did not encourage strongly enough students' willingness to challenge contemporary mores. Indeed, it was only in adulthood that people stood a chance of developing the ego strength to break free from prevailing opinion. "To really understand the problems in these fields," Fromm (1956) wrote, "a person must have had a great deal more experience in living than he has had at college age. For many people the age of 30 or 40 is much more appropriate for learning" (p. 346). Yet as students and faculty who have worked within cohort-style, accelerated learning programs that require student participation indicate, the desire to escape from the freedom of having to construct one's own curriculum is very strong (Baptiste and Brookfield, 1997; De Avila and others, 2000). Accelerated, participatory cohort programs contain their own pressures to automaton conformity.

Automaton conformity is pervasive and invisible. Like fish unaware of the water in which they live, citizens swim unsuspectingly in the ocean of conformity. People are surrounded by an "atmosphere of subtle suggestion which actually pervades our whole social life. . . . One never suspects that there is any order which one is expected to follow" (Fromm, 1956, p. 190). Under the enveloping influence of automaton conformity, "the individual ceases to be himself; he adopts entirely the kind of personality offered to him by cultural patterns and he . . . becomes exactly as all others are and as they expect him to be" (pp. 208–209). Any anxiety people might feel about this kind of existence concerns whether they are sufficiently assiduous in pursuing and realizing the pattern of conformity. The automaton conformist's credo can be summarized thus: "I must conform, not be different, not 'stick out'; I must be ready and willing to change according to the changes in the pattern; I must not ask whether I am right or wrong, but whether I am adjusted, whether I am not 'peculiar', not different" (Fromm, 1956, p. 153). Traditional education's emphasis on extended periods of teacher-directed, face-to-face group learning underscores the power of anonymous authority. It takes a separation from this face-to-face modality for people to stand any chance of developing a critical stance. Although Fromm did not specifically address anything like accelerated learning formats, the logic of his analysis of automaton conformity is clear. Extended periods of face-to-face learning constitute an ideal crucible for the successful perpetuation of automaton conformity.

However, it is not as simple as automaton conformity being evident only within traditional adult education structures. The phenomenon of automaton conformity can clearly be seen in the kind of cohort-style programs that are so popular with some advocates of accelerated learning (such as myself). Yet the possibility of automaton conformity is rarely addressed in discussions of cohort-style accelerated programs. The assumption of many involved in accelerated learning seems to be that a cohort represents an inherently supportive learning community that exhibits a concern for each member's welfare. But one of the dark sides of the cohort format is the unacknowledged possibility of automaton conformity. In accelerated cohort programs that involve a degree of participation, even of student governance, there is a danger that a few strong voices will define the agenda early on in the cohort's history and that this agenda will mimic the dominant culture's ideology. Alternatively, when students meet as a group free from faculty interference to decide on which curricular or policy demands, requests, or preferences they wish to present to faculty, there is the risk that dissenting minority voices will be seen as obstructive, as getting in the way of a speedy resolution. Students' desire to come to consensus and thereby present a united front to faculty overrides the need to be alert to implicit pressures for ideological conformity. (For interesting perspectives on how it feels to be participants in an accelerated learning cohort doctoral program in adult education in which students have a role in governance of the program, see Baptiste and Brookfield, 1997; De Avila and others, 2000; and Colin and Heaney, 2001.)

Accelerated Learning as a Site for Critical Adult Education

The connotations of commodification of accelerated learning and its image as a revenue-driven response to the need to claim an ever larger share of the adult student market seem on the face of it to make such learning an unlikely site for any kind of critical practice. Yet in two ways identified in this chapter, accelerated learning potentially holds advantages over more traditional programs that have greater contact hours and longer time spans. First, the fact that most study time in an accelerated learning program is spent in isolated work, with occasional short bursts of teacher-led group learning, means that learners experience a greater amount of isolation, privacy, and distance in their learning than is normally the case. Of course, there is nothing inherently liberating about detachment; one can independently pursue a course of study well within the guidelines established by the dominant culture, all the while assiduously engaging in self-censorship to ensure one does not go "off the rails." But Marcuse's point is that in a learner's detachment from the need to meet with others at a defined place and time lies a potentially revolutionary opening. Without some period of separation from peers, teachers, and culture, adults will mimic unthinkingly the views and preferences of the majority. Second, deprived of the usual weekly initiation into the typical adult classroom, the learner is less likely to be enveloped by the tentacles of anonymous authority. The authority of imagined common sense, public opinion, and conventional wisdom is mentally ingrained, it is true, but it is also reinforced each time learners come together in a classroom to find that the authority of official knowledge is once again underscored. When learners are stripped of this weekly two-hour classroom initiation, they are more likely to explore, or at least be open to, diverse perspectives that stand against the kind of pseudo-thinking whereby the learner simply paraphrases what she feels others are thinking or want to think.

An adult educational illustration of the connection between the kind of privacy fostered by the reduced contact time evident in many accelerated programs and the development of rebellious subjectivity is Cale and Huber's analysis (2001) of two attempts to create in adult learners a critical perspective on dominant, racist ideology. As part of this study, Huber summarizes a distance teacher education course focused on understanding diversity and promoting antiracist practice. This course was run as a fast-track summer institute with no requirement for students to meet for either formal classes or informal study. Huber records the surprising fact that "the assignments students completed that were most thoughtful and critical of their own positions of power were the ones that were completed alone" (Cale and Huber, 2001, p. 15). In these assignments, students "discussed openly the racism and sexism that they experienced in their families, their lack of contact with people of color, and their own passive racism" (p. 15). However, when these same learners formed an informal study group to work collaboratively on confronting racism, "the autonomous learning and thinking that manifested itself during their self-study disappeared after they completed the next two assignments together" (p. 15). As a consequence, "students who openly addressed the inherent racism in their classrooms and expressed a desire to end the racist practices that were a part of their hidden and overt curriculum did not complete a significant plan for change within their classrooms" (p. 15). Huber suggests that dominant ideology reproduced itself automatically in the informal group setting, whereas it could be kept temporarily at bay when participants inhabited the private space of autonomous, distanced thought. Huber's research prompts a reappraisal of the role of isolation and reduced contact with teachers and peers in developing a critical perspective. If distance, separation, and individual privacy are necessary conditions for adults to detach themselves from dominant ideology, then we must take more seriously the idea that accelerated learning can be a crucible for critical adult education rather than a compromised exercise in technical reductionism.

References

De Avila, E. B., and others. "Learning Democracy/Democratizing Learning: Participatory Graduate Education." In P. Campbell and B. Burnaby (eds.), *Participatory Practices in Adult Education*. Mahwah, N.J.: Erlbaum, 2000.

Baptiste, I., and Brookfield, S. D. ""Your So-Called Democracy Is Hypocritical Because You Can Always Fail Us: Learning and Living Democratic Contradictions in Graduate Adult Education." In P. Armstrong (ed.), *Crossing Borders, Breaking Boundaries: Research in the Education of Adults*. London: University of London, 1997.

Cale, G., and Huber, S. "Teaching the Oppressor to Be Silent: Conflicts in the 'Democratic' Classroom." In X. Coulter (ed.), *The Changing Face of Adult Learning*. Proceedings of the Twenty-First Annual Alliance/ACE Conference, Austin, Tex., October 10–13, 2001. Sarasota Springs, N.Y.: SUNY Empire State College.

Colin, S.A.J., III, and Heaney, T. "Negotiating the Democratic Classroom." In C. A. Hansman and P. A. Sissel (eds.), *Understanding and Negotiating the Political Landscape of Adult Education*. New Directions for Adult and Continuing Education, no. 91. San Francisco: Jossey-Bass, 2001.

Fromm, E. *Escape from Freedom*. New York: Holt, 1941.

Fromm, E. *The Sane Society*. London: Routledge, Kegan, 1956.

Marcuse, H. *One Dimensional Man*. Boston: Beacon Press, 1964.

Marcuse, H. *Counterrevolution and Revolt*. Boston: Beacon Press, 1972.

Marcuse, H. *The Aesthetic Dimension: Toward a Critique of Marxist Aesthetics*. Boston: Beacon Press, 1978.

STEPHEN D. BROOKFIELD *is Distinguished Professor at the University of St. Thomas, Minneapolis-St. Paul, Minnesota.*

8

Student learning is the major test of a program's quality, regardless of whether it is delivered in a traditional or accelerated format. Administrators and teachers in accelerated programs will increase effectiveness and build credibility by making sure that their programs employ best practices, measure results, and use assessment data for program improvement.

Accelerated and Traditional Formats: Using Learning as a Criterion for Quality

Craig Swenson

It is probably unfortunate that at some point in the past, the adjective *accelerated* was coupled to the noun *learning* to describe the instructional structures and formats discussed in this volume. "Accelerated" learning suggests that there is a "normal" method and pace for teaching and learning. It further implies that the traditional formats and methods employed in the academy embody the norm. Therefore, any method that deviates from this standard is likely to be treated with suspicion and may invite summary dismissal of what might otherwise be an effective, innovative approach to designing instruction. It is this scenario that will continue to make quality in design, instruction, and learning assessment so crucial for practitioners.

In the early 1990s, the leaders of the Weatherhead School of Business at Case Western Reserve University reengineered their M.B.A. program. They memorialized the experience in *Innovations in Professional Education* (Boyatzis and others, 1995) and titled their last chapter, "What If Learning Were the Purpose of Education?" Why so provocative a question? They recognized that the structure and design of instruction predominantly practiced in U.S. higher education was not adopted as the standard because it produced learning in students. Learning, to be perfectly frank, had little to do with it. Our dominant instructional practice and structure—respectively, the lecture and the semester—arose for reasons unrelated to student learning. Our dependence on these two conventions is based on flawed pedagogical assumptions.

New Directions for Adult and Continuing Education, no. 97, Spring 2003 © Wiley Periodicals, Inc.

The lecture is but one of a variety of methods in an excellent teacher's repertoire. Sadly, the lecture appears to have become the principal, or in some cases the sole, means of instruction employed in many college and university classrooms. This practice implies that learning is primarily an act of transmitting information from the expert to passive, empty vessels. Furthermore, although a lecture may be the most economical way to deliver instruction by the few to the many (try imagining most colleges and universities being able to balance their books without large lecture halls filled with undergraduates), the truth is that most of us remember remarkably little of what we heard in these settings.

We accept the semester or quarter as the appropriate length of a course for similar reasons. It is easy to forget that they were inventions of a different time. Academic calendars designed for an agrarian society are anachronisms in the digital age, where more than half of all students work full-time, year-round, and instruction can take place regardless of time and place.

All Learning Is Individual

The inference drawn from current practice—that these methods are the acceptable way to structure or format learning or that there is a single acceptable way—is flawed. This is so because all learning at its core is individual. This is not to say that the epistemology of learning is not social (that is, that what we can know and our ways of knowing are situated in the contexts of our social lives). It does suggest that the process by which each person learns best is individual—and not only individual but also situational. A learner's preferred learning style, dominant perceptual mode, role, motivation, interest in the subject matter, and other variables combine to make every individual learning transaction a universe of one.

The obvious lesson is that teaching formats and structures do not guarantee results. Teaching is neither a necessary nor sufficient condition to ensure that learning occurs. One need only call to mind a great autodidact like Lincoln to be reminded that so much of what we learn over the course of our lives takes place independent of teachers (at least as we think of education) and outside formal, structured education and training programs. Given this knowledge, it seems odd that so many in higher education look askance at prior learning assessment programs for adult learners. The "unless you learned it in my class, the way I learned it when I was a student, you didn't learn it" brand of arrogance can still be found in higher education, and that attitude raises a significant challenge to accelerated learning programs.

Challenging Conventional Wisdom

In any field, especially one in which tradition is as entrenched as it is in higher education, innovation and change do not occur easily or without struggle. Entire systems have been constructed to codify and then protect conventional ways of doing things. In most organizational systems, support functions tend to take on lives of their own that become independent of the practices they were meant to support. People rooted in those systems often share an interest in preserving the status quo for reasons having nothing to do with the primary purpose of the activity.

Conversely, pressure for innovation in higher education usually comes from those who set out to serve the needs of new and diverse student populations. And it usually comes from the realization that traditional means of instruction and program design are inadequate. In seeking to do things differently, innovators regularly find themselves at odds with colleagues, administrators, regulators, and accreditors. Teachers and administrators in divisions of continuing education and those in nontraditional institutions are often condescended to by their skeptical colleagues in other disciplines. The irony is that most of those who so casually dismiss accelerated programs have failed to question whether the traditional system works well enough to provide the benchmark for comparison.

The role of quality in accelerated learning programs should be no different than it is in traditional programs. It seems that as long as a class is scheduled for fifty minutes five times a week, for sixteen weeks, there is an implicit assumption that learning is occurring. If we hope to establish the legitimacy of accelerated learning programs, we must be willing to engage in discussion around the conventions that govern current practice. Only in this way will we be able to influence accrediting standards and regulations that use those conventions to define appropriate learning structures and formats.

Stephen Brookfield (1987) defines critical thinking as a process that involves accepting that our behaviors are based on assumptions, recognizing that our assumptions are contextual, and then challenging the bases of those assumptions. Traditional higher education has based some of its standard practices on assumptions that beg for examination.

Such an analysis is essential if we hope to adopt new structures for promoting and facilitating learning—practices that could make a positive difference in the lives of adult and younger learners alike. Adherence to the traditional academic calendar offers a useful illustration. Because of the complexity of their lives and multiple life roles they assume, adult learners often place a high premium on their time. They list such convenience variables as schedule, location, and time to degree as significant factors in their choice of an institution (Aslanian, 2001). For many, the significant time periods between semesters may represent lost time that they could put to more productive use in achieving personal and professional goals.

Quality in Accelerated Learning: An Operational Definition

If learning is truly the purpose of education, defining educational quality becomes all the more crucial because quality practices should lead to learning. The truth is that learning in the traditional system is often serendipitous.

Learning that takes place during a course I teach may occur in spite of, rather than because of, something I have done. This is a sure antidote to hubris in a teacher. Boyatzis and others (1995) offer this sobering reminder:

> It is a mistake to assume that teaching and learning are the same thing: What you teach is not necessarily what I learn, and what I learn may be other than what you teach. . . . Education has tended to focus on teaching; often assuming rather than promoting it. . . .
> You can lead students to an experience, but you cannot make them learn. Engaging their views and ways of knowing appears fundamental to stimulating their motivation and desire to learn [pp. 234–235].

Luckily for those of us who make our living by teaching, learning *does* occur in formal settings; for some learners, it actually happens as a result of something we do. There are times when the variables all work together within the setting and the style of the teacher, and the result is student learning. Sadly, though, although all the learners in my classes are capable of learning, not all do.

When I am armed with this knowledge, my goal as a teacher or administrator becomes to create the conditions under which the greatest amount of learning can take place within the greatest number of learners. This statement provides the basis for an operational definition of quality in accelerated learning programs—in any academic structure, for that matter. Student learning, not inputs, becomes the metric by which success is judged. At the end of an independent lesson, group class meeting, course, or program, we must be able to answer two questions: Do learners know what they should know? Can they do what they should be able to do? It was this insight that formed the basis for Barr and Tagg's call (1995) for a paradigm shift from teaching to learning.

It also led to the insight offered by Boyatzis and others (1995) that we must view the job of teaching differently than we normally do. Instead of being transmitters of information, teachers must come to see themselves as managers of the learning process. This is especially true in accelerated learning programs, where we often have less time. When learning becomes the goal, parity in expectations between traditional and accelerated instruction becomes possible.

There is now increasing pressure to change the system that assumes quality based on inputs without outcomes. For example, regional accrediting associations have begun to establish criteria that require institutions to develop learning assessment programs. This is still at the early stages because, as Ewell (2001) points out, most require only that programs to assess learning exist—not that they demonstrate that students actually learned. Advances in electronic technology and the proliferation of distance-learning programs are helping to convince accreditors and regulators of the weakness of the Carnegie Unit as a quality measure. Until these changes become institutionalized, innovators will still shoulder the greater burden of demonstrating equivalence.

Designing for Quality

Engineering quality into learning environments and measuring learning outcomes are ways to increase the acceptability of new learning formats and structures. Other measures, such as student persistence, graduation, and transfer rates, are also important indicators of institutional effectiveness, but students ostensibly may persist, graduate, or transfer without having learned what they should have learned. In addition, it does not follow that simply because learners were able to learn more efficiently in a specific accelerated format, that all accelerated learning formats are effective. We must be willing to isolate, to the degree possible, the conditions and methods that account for the learning effectiveness of those successful formats. That knowledge makes it more possible for programs being created to be pre-evaluated in relation to the use of these best practices.

This process of creating successful programs becomes easier, more credible, and more successful when faculty members and administrators responsible for them approach design, implementation, and evaluation with the following considerations in mind.

The best time to decide how any program should be evaluated is before it is implemented. If we hope to have accelerated learning innovations accepted, the best way is to approach the task from a scholarly perspective: we want to try something new, we want to know whether it is effective, and we are willing to go where our data lead us. In addition, there is an adage from the world of business that applies here: "If you can't measure it, you can't manage it." Academicians sometimes bristle at this kind of rhetoric. They will respond, "Not everything that counts can be counted." That may be true, but there are many things that count that can be counted, and if we can, we ought to. Only by doing this kind of assessment and evaluation will innovators gain acceptance for their efforts.

One activity taught to facilitators in quality management programs is to get team members to describe the desired end by asking, "What would *good* look like?" The discipline of clearly envisioning and articulating outcomes is essential in gaining acceptance and credibility for our programs. It helps us define quality. We must be able to describe what, at the end of the accelerated learning experience or program, our students should know or be able to do. This approach may seem so basic to experienced practitioners as not to require repeating. However, new teachers or trainers of adults sometimes become so enamored with methods and techniques that they forget why they are using them.

Once the objectives for a program of study and the derivative objectives for each course or learning experience that make up the program are identified, they should be clearly articulated to everyone involved in the program: faculty members or trainers, students or participants, and administrators or managers. In a meta-analysis of the literature related to goal setting and task performance, Locke, Shaw, Saari, and Latham (1981) conclude that "the beneficial effect of goal setting on task performance is

one of the most robust and replicable findings in the psychological literature" (p. 145). In 90 percent of studies, specific and challenging goals led
to higher performance: "Goals affect performance by directing attention,
mobilizing effort, increasing persistence, and motivating strategy development" (p. 125). Developing clear and challenging learning objectives can
have the same effect in our programs. When objectives are clear, measur-
able, and explicit and are communicated to all, participants will work
together for their achievement.

Over the past eighteen months in my institution, the deans and academic program councils have undertaken a process of reengineering our
learning assessment programs. Together they established a new set of
university-wide learning goals that describe the general knowledge and competencies that should be developed across the curriculum in every program.
For programs such as education, nursing, or counseling, where professional
practice may proceed from specific theoretical perspectives, the program
councils have also developed conceptual frameworks—descriptions of the
theoretical foundations on which the programs are built.

The councils then identified terminal objectives for each program.
These objectives represent the discipline-specific knowledge and skills that
graduates should possess. A fresh view was taken of the courses and experiences that are part of existing academic programs in order to determine
whether their content contributed to the achievement of the terminal objectives. Program objectives were mapped to courses within the program to
ensure that all terminal objectives, and all derivative objectives that would
lead to the achievement of the terminal objectives, were in place and consistent. In some cases, courses were retired and others created. In other
cases, existing courses were changed to add missing content or remove
superfluous or unnecessary material.

With this foundation in place, we believe we have become even more
able to judge the success of our programs in producing graduates who know
what they should know and can do what they should be able to do. It gives
deans and program councils the information they need to create summative
assessments of student learning. It also helps individual instructors to
understand how the courses they teach fit into the larger picture. This
makes them better able to develop and administer formative classroom
assessments and adapt instruction to learner needs and the achievement of
course objectives.

The additional benefit, perhaps most important to accelerated learning
programs, is that this kind of structure allows for comparisons. Because we
know specifically what we are trying to accomplish, we are better able to
demonstrate the equivalence of classroom-based programs, an on-line program, and a program that uses a blended-delivery format. We can also compare different formats, where applicable, against nationally normed
assessments for professional licensure. Finally, the results of these assessments provide data that can be used for improvement.

Engineer Best Practice into Accelerated Programs

We already know a great deal about what works and does not when it comes to designing instruction, even though most college and university classrooms do not reflect that knowledge. On the other hand, a mark of quality in accelerated learning programs is that they will employ instructional best practices. By doing so, we strengthen the likelihood that learners will achieve the desired learning outcomes. If the old lecture-test paradigm is ill fitted to the traditional classroom, it is even more out of place in an accelerated learning format.

It is not possible here to provide an exhaustive list of quality practices for accelerated programs. What follows, however, is a short list of questions based on some of those best practices. These may be useful as we review or create accelerated learning programs for adult learners. There are numerous good sources. Chickering and Gamson's "Seven Principles for Good Practice in Undergraduate Education" (1987) is a good basis for comparison and reflected in this list. Brookfield (1992) offered generalizations about adult learners that also provide valuable food for thought. Process theories, such as Kolb's experiential learning cycle (1984), are useful, as are numerous others. Many other examples could be cited. What follows here is a sample distilled from some of those many sources:

• *Does instruction require learners to be actively involved in their own learning?* Instruction that treats adult learners as active participants in the learning process is more likely to result in the achievement of learning objectives. Do they understand the objectives? Do they get to help set some of the objectives? Are they expected and encouraged to offer opinions, share ideas, make presentations? By encouraging active involvement, we tap into the affective realm, thus engaging the learner's interest and deepening the learning context and experience. This provides greater cognitive engagement and retention of knowledge. The Scottish philosopher Hume ([1793] 2000) wrote, "Reason is and aught to be the slave of the passions. Reason can tell us what to do, only the passions can *will* us to do it."

• *Does instruction make use of the learner's life and work experience?* The primary difference between younger and adult learners is the amount of experience they bring to the classroom. Brookfield (1986), Knowles (1990), and others argue that adults learn best when they build bridges between new knowledge and past experience. A learner's past experience and current life roles and responsibilities provide the context through which they are better able to make meaning from new information. This notion also inspired Freire's early work (1970) in adult literacy. This experiential context can make it possible for adults to learn more efficiently. Quality accelerated learning programs make use of this knowledge by placing activities, assignments, and assessments in the context of the adult's life and work.

• *Does instruction allow adequate time for reflection?* Brookfield (1992) notes that despite our emphasis on praxis in adult learning, many adults in academic programs report frustration at how thick and fast new information comes at them without adequate time to reflect. Kolb (1984), who lists reflective observation as one of the steps in his experiential learning model, suggests that it is the step that is too often given short shrift. It may seem incongruous to suggest that an antecedent of quality in accelerated learning programs is time for reflection, but it can be argued that reflection is even more important when instruction follows an intensive format.

Providing adequate time for reflection can be accomplished in a variety of ways. Reflection is a natural by-product of placing assignments and activities in the context of learners' current roles and past experience, as suggested in the question as to whether instruction makes use of the learner's life and work experience. Journaling is another useful tool. Using critical incident techniques in advance of a lecture or activity and then requiring learners to apply the new knowledge to the referent experience is another. Well-designed small group breakouts allow learners to reflect together. Informal assignments that encourage learners to reflect on the most important concepts, apply that learning at the workplace or other context, and share this learning the next time the class meets is a way to close the loop on the learning process. Even requiring learners to reflect for several moments before allowing questions to be answered in a discussion can foster reflection and enhance the important process of making connections and seeing relationships.

An important caveat is that in order to ensure that this approach is integral to a program, faculty members selected to provide instruction in accelerated learning programs for adults need to subscribe to this philosophy of instruction, be trained in it, and be reinforced for modeling it in the classroom. There is plenty of room for individual style and interpretation, which may be applied differently in an organizational behavior versus a statistics course, but agreement as to the underlying principle is essential to achievement of the optimal amount of learning in an accelerated program.

• *Does the program individualize instruction to the greatest possible degree?* When we accept that learning ultimately takes place at the level of the individual learner, the best possible approach is to perform a comprehensive assessment of every learner. We identify their preferred learning styles and dominant perceptual modes. We assess their entering levels of knowledge and skills for each subject. We might even try to make a judgment about their level of interest and affective involvement in a subject. This profile would enable us to design a specialized course of study for that learner. We would create an individual learning plan around a particular subject and provide instruction or learning experiences to identified learning objectives. Finally, we would assess the learner's mastery of the objectives and adapt further instruction to overcome gaps in mastery.

This approach is certainly possible but not economically feasible. In the P-12 arena, for example, the Sylvan-type model does provide individualized instruction, but at a cost that almost certainly exceeds the resources of publicly financed educational systems and all but a very few private systems. In higher education, this has been one of the goals of Western Governors University, though it has yet to find widespread support for the competency-based degrees. Other nontraditional institutions, like Excelsior and Thomas Edison, have also built models that individualize credentialing.

Furthermore, although advancements in instructional and communications technology offer the promise that costs may come down, this kind of approach to learning goes against the grain of the traditional academy. Most higher education institutions achieve economic feasibility by taking measures to decrease instructional unit costs. Increasing the number of students in front of a faculty member does this. The more bodies seated in a lecture hall, the less the cost per hour of instruction. But it is not just cost that drives this model. Tradition accounts for much of the "this is the way we do things because this is the way we have always done things" approach to instruction. Education is validated through completion of a course or a program rather than through a demonstration of students' knowledge.

Conversely, accelerated learning programs for adults are generally based on the understanding that learners' time is at a premium and that time to degree is an important consideration in program choice. One of the most wasteful conventions of higher education is making learners take courses where they already have the requisite knowledge. It was this detriment that drove the creation of prior learning assessment programs. Quality accelerated learning programs use this process but adhere to accepted guidelines, such as those developed by the Council on Adult and Experiential Learning.

In addition, quality programs seek to measure the knowledge and skills of entering learners to make certain that they are at least minimally equipped to participate successfully in the program of study. Finally, these programs will help faculty members become skilled in classroom assessment so that they will be able to assess the entry knowledge, skill levels, and degree of learner engagement in the subject being studied. With this knowledge, teachers are able to adapt instruction appropriately to the level of their students.

Conclusion

The title of this chapter may suggest that something about accelerated programs suggests a need for a higher standard for quality than programs offered in a traditional way. In reality, there should be no differences in expectation regarding quality practices or outcomes. There is a perceived difference, however, and innovative educators will continue to bear the burden of demonstrating quality until learning becomes the purpose of education and formats are judged by how much learning takes place.

The goal should be to create the conditions under which the greatest amount of learning can take place within the greatest number of learners. This requires that we decide together "what good looks like" and agree on the purposes and terminal objectives of a degree, course of study, course, or learning experience. This requires deciding what it is that learners should know and be able to do at the end of the experience.

In designing accelerated programs to achieve these learning objectives, it is essential to employ practices that research has demonstrated are most likely to produce learning effectively and efficiently. Instruction that requires adult learners to be actively involved in their own learning, requires collaboration with others, makes use of their greater life and work experience, allows adequate opportunity for reflection, and attempts to individualize instruction is more likely to achieve proficient learning outcomes.

The key to future success will be in demonstrating that accelerated learning programs are as effective in producing learning outcomes as traditional programs are. The difficulty posed is that traditional programs often do not provide baseline measurements for comparison. It may seem ironic, but it is likely that the pressure that accelerated learning practitioners feel to demonstrate the effectiveness of their programs will be a significant force for change in traditional programs. A well-conceived learning outcomes assessment program, which uses data for curriculum and instructional improvement, is essential to improving higher education—and to silencing skeptics of accelerated programs.

References

Aslanian, C. *Adult Students Today.* New York: College Board, 2001.

Barr, R. B., and Tagg, J. "From Learning to Teaching: A New Paradigm for Undergraduate Education." *Change,* 1995, 27(6), 13–25.

Boyatzis, R. E., and others. *Innovation in Professional Education: Steps on a Journey from Teaching to Learning.* San Francisco: Jossey-Bass, 1995.

Brookfield, S. D. "Universal Experiences of Adult Learners." Paper presented at the Lifelong Learning Conference, National University, San Diego, Calif., Jan. 16–18, 1992.

Brookfield, S. D. *Understanding and Facilitating Adult Learning.* San Francisco: Jossey-Bass, 1986.

Brookfield, S. D. *Developing Critical Thinkers: Challenging Adults to Explore Alternative Ways of Thinking and Acting.* San Francisco: Jossey-Bass, 1987.

Chickering, A., and Gamson, Z. F. "Seven Principles for Good Practice in Undergraduate Education." *AAHE Bulletin,* 1987, 39(7), 3–7.

Ewell, P. T. *Accreditation and Student Learning Outcomes: A Proposed Point of Departure.* Washington, D.C.: Council on Higher Education Accreditation, 2001.

Freire, P. *The Pedagogy of the Oppressed.* New York: Continuum, 1970.

Hume, D. *A Treatise of Human Nature.* Oxford: Oxford University Press, 2000. (Originally published 1793.)

Knowles, M. S. *The Adult Learner: A Neglected Species.* (4th ed.). Houston: Gulf Publishing Company, 1990.

Kolb, D. A. *Experiential Learning.* Upper Saddle River, N.J.: Prentice Hall, 1984.

Locke, E. A., Shaw, K. N., Saari, L. M., and Latham, G. P. "Goal Setting and Task Performance: 1969–1980." *Psychological Bulletin,* 1981, 90(1), 125–152.

CRAIG SWENSON *is provost and senior vice president for academic affairs at University of Phoenix.*

9

This chapter explores the future of accelerated learning as an innovative force within higher education.

Accelerated Learning: Future Roles and Influences

Raymond J. Wlodkowski, Carol E. Kasworm

According to an often-told story, when Franklin Roosevelt died in 1945, it was Eleanor Roosevelt who told Harry Truman of his death. He was so stunned that initially he said nothing. When he did break the silence, he asked Mrs. Roosevelt if there were anything he might do for her. She is said to have replied, "Is there anything we can do for you? For you are the one in trouble now."

This story touches on a fact of history that provides insight into the role of accelerated learning in higher education. Harry Truman was initially seen as inadequate and undeserving to be president. In the light of the role of the presidency, he was perceived to be inferior, someone to be joked about. He was judged to be a provincial product of big city politics destined by forces beyond his control to stand in the shadow of the popular patrician leader he replaced. With time, possibly thirty years after Truman's presidency, he came to be seen as a very good president and reformer with policies that presciently shaped the world. In an analogous sense, is this not where accelerated learning stands relative to traditional learning in higher education—where Truman stood relative to Roosevelt on April 12, 1945: a very unlikely successor who appears to many of those in power as unworthy of the responsibility and task ahead?

Accelerated learning specifically and adult education generally have made enormous inroads into higher education because they are moneymakers. They did not gain a place in this arena because they were homes to prestigious researchers or famous scholars. They took hold in higher education because of the demographic momentum of adults whose numbers and demand for continuing learning could not be ignored. Business management, teacher education, and computer science are the academic fields where non-traditional learners, largely adults, are applying for admission in numbers that are startling in their magnitude. Seventy-three percent of all college students today are nontraditional learners (National Center for Education Statistics, 2002). Add to this fact the needs of an information society, proliferating distance-learning venues and continuing advances of computer technology are changing the face of higher education.

Roots

Accelerated learning is an outgrowth of adult education, whose legacy has had an enormous influence on the shape and trajectory of accelerated learning. As a field of study, adult education has been more doctrinaire and pragmatic than traditional education, where a very strong research and theoretical orientation hold sway. Leading thinkers in adult education, such as Paulo Freire, Phyllis Cunningham, and Jack Mezirow, have tended to be activists and advocates of social and personal transformation. They espouse a more egalitarian worldview than the philosopher-king perspective so common to classical and traditional education.

With this background, adult educators who have led the growth of accelerated learning programs would be far more at ease eschewing the lecture method of teaching for the active learning method of teaching; trying flexible schedules instead of fifty-minute classes in the daytime; respecting adult experience as a means to inform teaching and research rather than vice versa; using adjunct faculty from the workforce as the main conduit of learning rather than full-time faculty housed at a university; and embracing new technology for teaching rather than shunning it as bothersome and unnecessary.

Once such boundaries were broken in adult education and there were people to fill the classes, it was predictable that time, the magistrate of tradition, would be assaulted. As pointed out in Chapter One, the research to support a fixed relationship between time and learning is scant and questionable. Do we really need sixteen weeks and forty-five clock hours to learn a body of knowledge or skills that are not standardized and consistently taught or assessed in the first place? And if we place learning in the forefront of the college experience and use effective assessment procedures to determine quality and sustain improvement, as Barbara Walvoord (in Chapter Four) and Craig Swenson (in Chapter Eight) suggest, would we not have a pathway to shorten the time for learning that is a responsible action? Questions such as these have easily led adult educators to accelerated learning.

One more question is important: Who benefits? Because the foreground for discussion of accelerated learning has so often been economic and because the largest university that offers accelerated learning is the University of Phoenix, a for-profit institution, the primary beneficiaries that receive media attention are the institutions themselves and their coffers, enriched through the exploitation of an abundant adult market. However, as Carol Kasworm (in Chapter Two), Patricia Scott (in Chapter Three), and Elise Burton (in Chapter Six) discussed, adult learners are discriminating as well as transformed students who appear grateful for their accelerated courses and programs. If one of the major purposes of higher education is accessibility and learning opportunity for deserving students, then accelerated learning programs are answering the call. As indicated in Chapter One, when we look at the adult students and use criteria such as income, gender, and race and ethnicity, they tend to be women whose lower family income and race and ethnicity are underrepresented in mainstream traditional colleges.

Roles

Probably the most productive and effective role that accelerated learning can play in higher education is as an ally with traditional education. Recognizing that both entities want an excellent education and relevant success for the diverse body of people in this country, accelerated learning fills a much-needed niche: nontraditional learners who are often working more than twenty hours a week and have families and other responsibilities that do not permit residential full-time learning experiences.

There is also much to share with each other. The facilities, buildings, laboratories, research capacity, and specialization at many traditional universities are exceptional. In terms of experience with flexibility, scheduling, advanced use of technology for teaching, educational and assessment innovations, teaching nontraditional students, and resource utilization, accelerated degree programs also have much to offer. Creating hybrids of any sort between traditional and accelerated learning programs has been only minimally explored.

Probably a role being played less intentionally by accelerated learning is that of reformer. There is evidence that accelerated learning programs are more effective with nontraditional learners, operate at significantly lower costs, and have similar or better learning outcomes. These results raise questions by legislators and citizenry regarding more expensive and restrictive higher education practices. By virtue of their popularity and success, accelerated programs have drawn into question the need for large bodies of full-time faculty, minimal teaching and advising loads, residential learning, need for additional campus buildings, inadequate use of technology for teaching, traditional student selection criteria, and the validity and reliability of traditional college testing procedures, including the Scholastic Aptitude Test and Graduate Record Exam measures.

Yet accelerated learning programs have their own issues to consider in a reform agenda. With shorter time schedules for learning, there is less margin for error. Quality of course instruction, as Patricia Scott points out, can be poor. There is a need to monitor courses and learning outcomes closely.

There may be disciplines of learning such as the physical sciences and types of students such as those who are weak in self-regulation skills who are not appropriate candidates for accelerated learning programs. With profits as significant as those generally reported, institutions housing accelerated programs have a fiduciary responsibility to conduct scrupulous self-study and research.

There is also the commercialization of learning aspect as Brookfield pointed out. When schools financially profit from more students taking more courses and graduating more quickly, there is reason to be alert for potential abuse of this kind of efficiency.

Public disclosure of assessment procedures, institutional data on retention and degree completion, grading policies, and curriculum content may need to be considered as requisite for accelerated degree programs. Proprietary rights may be strategically used by institutions with accelerated learning programs to hide questionable practices as well as to maintain a competitive edge.

The last role we offer for accelerated learning is in the form of a messenger in higher education—a messenger that signals that times have changed dramatically. By substance and responsiveness, accelerated degree learning programs present these signs:

- A for-profit, accelerated degree university with over 130,000 students
- On-line accelerated courses, with completion in typically half the time covering similar content and outcomes in traditional courses
- 250 colleges and universities with accelerated programs
- 13 percent of all adult students enrolled in accelerated degree programs (Aslanian, 2001)
- Universities with accelerated degree programs on four continents
- 73 percent of all students as nontraditional learners, who do not fit into the typical instructional delivery system of most institutions

Accelerated learning signals a tidal wave of change for higher education. Leaders in the field could shoot this messenger by ignoring the transformations that have occurred. But this response would be an irresponsible stance in the face of the great need for innovative support for adult learners in higher education. Perhaps more regressive is to stand silent to the mocking of these programs as "cash cow enterprises" or "drive-thru universities," terms that have become clichés and do not articulate the contributions emerging from accelerated learning.

It is still rare to see higher education journals, including the *Chronicle of Higher Education,* publishing articles that substantively discuss adult education, much less accelerated learning. This volume begins the first extensive discussion of accelerated learning as a major innovation in higher education. It not only predicts a changing future for higher education but invites a broader audience to a much closer scrutiny of the worth of accelerated learning as it contributes to this evolution. In this regard, our responsibility as adult educators in the field of accelerated learning is to effectively continue our work as we vigorously expand our research and judiciously disseminate our practices.

References

Aslanian, C. B. *Adult Students Today.* New York: College Board, 2001.

National Center for Education Statistics. *The Condition of Education 2002.* Washington, D.C.: U.S. Government Printing Office, 2002.

RAYMOND J. WLODKOWSKI is director of the Center for the Study of Accelerated Learning and professor in the School for Professional Studies at Regis University, Denver.

CAROL E. KASWORM is professor of adult education and department head of Adult and Community College Education at North Carolina State University, Raleigh.

INDEX

Abbott, R. D., 33

Accelerated degree learning: adult student experience in, 17–27; assessment of, 39–49; conceptual model of adult, 24*fig*–26; controversial aspects of, 7; criteria for successful, 52–54; critical theory perspective on, 73–82; defining, 6–7; engineering best practice into, 89–91; growing interest/increase in, 5–6, 51–52; high education role o, 95–97; institutional purpose of, 54–55; issues for further research on, 13–14; key elements in starting/maintaining/success of, 10–12, 54–60; marketing/promotional considerations of, 57–60; obstacles/barriers to, 60; programmatic decision processes and, 55; roots of, 94–95. *See also* Distance learning

Accelerated degree programs criteria: commitment of leadership as, 54; designed for adult learners, 52; excellent customer services, 54; learner-focused/market-sensitive approach, 52; passion for quality, 52–53; program accessibility, 53; variety of delivery options, 53

Accelerated learning: accelerated degree program elements supporting, 18; automaton conformity and, 79–80; as critical to adult education, 80–82; possibility of rebellious subjectivity and, 74–78; roots of, 94–95; student beliefs regarding accelerated programs and, 22–24. *See also* Learning

Accelerated learning program quality: accreditation and, 8; alumni attitudes and, 9–10; engineering curricular design for, 87–88; examining, 7–8; initial evidence regarding, 10; using learning as criterion for, 8–9, 83–92; operational definition of, 85–86; student attitudes and, 9

Accelerated learning program study (2001–2002): implications of, 12; important findings of, 11–12; two schools examined during, 10–11

Accreditation/quality relationship, 8

Active learning, 31

Adult action, 25

Adult competence, 24–25

Adult Learning Survey (2001), 10, 11

Adult student identity, 21–22

Adult students. *See* Students

Adult work identity, 25–26

Advertising of program, 59–60

Aggregated data example, 44*t*

Alexander, P., 65

Alumni/program quality relationship, 9–10

American Association of State Colleges and Universities, 10

Anderson, V. J., 43, 44

Animal Farm (Orwell), 73

Aslanian, C. B., 5, 12, 14, 85, 96

La Asociación Femenina Para El Desarrollo Rural (AFEDER), 67–68

La Asociación Nuestros Ahijados (Guatemala), 66, 70

Assessment: creating a practical guide for, 39–40; defining the research question for, 40–41; goal for, 50; improving program on basis of, 46–49; methodology for student performance, 41–46; responsibilities of program, 49*t*

Astin, A. W., 10, 11, 37

AT&T, 56

Atkinson, P., 64, 65, 66, 69

Automaton conformity, 79–80

Baptiste, I., 80

Barr, R. B., 86

Batra, M. M., 46

Baxter Magolda, M. B., 26

Billson, J. M., 33

Biology course: aggregated data on, 44*t*; learning goals assessment of, 47*t*

Blowers, S., 18

Bourne, G., 32

Boyatzis, R. E., 83, 86

Bray, D. M., 56

Brickell, H. M., 53

Brookfield, S. D., 3, 7, 73, 80, 82, 85, 89

Burton, E. M., 3, 63, 65, 71

Students (*continued*)
beliefs regarding accelerated programs and learning, 22–24; course evaluations by, 34; high-quality intensive courses and performance by, 36–37; instructor characteristics and learning by, 30–31; program information sessions offered to, 58–59; program quality and attitudes of, 9; reflections on accelerated programs by, 17–18; reflections on Dreamer Center program by, 67; SOFE cost issues for, 70; successful adult student identity by, 21–22; support of fellow, 20. *See also* Learners
Supportive learning world: accessible/relevant instructional program and, 18, 19; degree structure facilitating completion, 18, 19–20; program connecting student community, 18–19, 20; three characteristics of, 18–19
Swenson, C., 3, 83, 92, 94

Tagg, J., 86
Teaching: high-quality learning experience and, 31–33; learning experience and methods of, 31–33

Teaching Learning Technology Group, 46
Terenzini, P. T., 33
Tiberius, R. G., 33
Tinto, V., 12
Traub, J., 7
Truman, H., 93

University of Phoenix, 5

Validity issues, 42

Walberg, H. J., 8
Walvoord, B. E., 2, 39, 43, 44, 46, 50, 94
Weatherhead School of Business (Case Western Reserve University), 83
Weinstein, C. E., 31
Wenger, E., 20, 25
Westover, T., 7, 8, 9, 10, 29, 60
Wittrock, M. C., 31
Wlodkowski, R. J., 2, 3, 5, 6, 7, 8, 9, 10, 11, 15, 29, 49, 60, 93, 97
Wolfe, A., 7
Wulff, D. A., 33

Back Issue/Subscription Order Form

Copy or detach and send to:
Jossey-Bass, A Wiley Company, 989 Market Street, San Francisco CA 94103-1741

Call or fax toll-free: Phone 888-378-2537 6:30AM – 3PM PST; Fax 888-481-2665

Back Issues: Please send me the following issues at $27 each
(Important: please include ISBN number with your order.)

_____

_____

_____

$ _____   Total for single issues

$ _____   SHIPPING CHARGES: SURFACE   Domestic Canadian
                                          First Item $5.00 $6.00
                                          Each Add'l Item $3.00 $1.50
                 For next-day and second-day delivery rates, call the number listed above.

Subscriptions: Please _start _renew my subscription to *New Directions for Adult and Continuing Education* for the year 2_____ at the following rate:

U.S.	_ Individual $70	_ Institutional $149
Canada	_ Individual $70	_ Institutional $189
All Others	_ Individual $94	_ Institutional $223
Online Subscription		_ Institutional $149

**For more information about online subscriptions visit
www.interscience.wiley.com**

$ _____   Total single issues and subscriptions (Add appropriate sales tax for your state for single issue orders. No sales tax for U.S. subscriptions. Canadian residents, add GST for subscriptions and single issues.)

_ Payment enclosed (U.S. check or money order only)
_ VISA _MC _AmEx _Discover Card #_____ Exp. Date _____

Signature _____ Day Phone _____
_ Bill Me (U.S. institutional orders only. Purchase order required.)

Purchase order # _____
                 Federal Tax ID13559302   **GST 89102 8052**

Name _____

Address _____

_____

Phone _____ E-mail _____

For more information about Jossey-Bass, visit our Web site at www.josseybass.com

PROMOTION CODE ND03

ACE92 **Sociocultural Perspectives on Learning through Work**
Tara Fenwick
Offers an introduction to current themes among academic researchers who
are interested in sociocultural understandings of work-based learning and
working knowledge—how people learn in and through everyday activities
that they think of as work. Explores how learning is embedded in the social
relationships, cultural dynamics, and politics of work, and recommends
different ways for educators to be part of the process.
ISBN 0-7879-5775-5

ACE91 **Understanding and Negotiating the Political Landscape of Adult Education**
Catherine A. Hansman, Peggy A. Sissel
Provides key insights into the politics and policy issues in adult education
today. Offering effective strategies for reflection and action, chapters explore
issues in examination and negotiation of the political aspects of higher
education, adult educators in K–12-focused colleges of education, literacy
education, social welfare reform, professional organizations, and identity of
the field.
ISBN 0-7879-5775-5

ACE90 **Promoting Journal Writing in Adult Education**
Leona M. English, Marie A. Gillen
Exploring the potential for personal growth and learning through journal
writing for student and mentor alike, this volume aims to establish journal
writing as an integral part of the teaching and learning process. Offers
examples of how journal writing can be, and has been, integrated into
educational areas as diverse as health education, higher education, education
for women, and English as a Second Language.
ISBN 0-7879-5774-7

ACE89 **The New Update on Adult Learning Theory**
Sharan B. Merriam
A companion work to 1993's popular An Update on Adult Learning Theory,
this issue examines the developments, research, and continuing scholarship
in self-directed learning. Exploring context-based learning, informal and
incidental learning, somatic learning, and narrative learning, the authors
analyze recent additions to well-established theories and discuss the
potential impact of today's cutting-edge approaches.
ISBN 0-7879-5773-9

ACE88 **Strategic Use of Learning Technologies**
Elizabeth J. Burge
The contributors draw on case examples to explore the advantages and
disadvantages of three existing learning technologies—print, radio, and the
Internet—and examine how a large urban university has carefully combined
old and new technologies to provide a range of learner services tailored to its
enormous and varied student body.
ISBN 0-7879-5426-8

ACE87 **Team Teaching and Learning in Adult Education**
Mary-Jane Eisen, Elizabeth J. Tisdell
The contributors show how team teaching can increase both organizational
and individual learning in settings outside of a traditional classroom, such as
a recently deregulated public utility, a national literacy organization, and

community-based settings such as Chicago's south side. They discuss how team teaching can be used in colleges and universities, describing strategies for administrators and teachers who want to integrate it into their curricula and classrooms.
ISBN 0-7879-5425-X

ACE86　Charting a Course for Continuing Professional Education: Reframing Professional Practice
Vivian W. Mott, Barbara J. Daley
This volume offers a resource to help practitioners examine and improve professional practice, and set new directions for the field of CPE across multiple professions. The contributors provide a brief review of the development of the field of CPE, analyze significant issues and trends that are shaping and changing the field, and propose a vision of the future of CPE.
ISBN 0-7879-5424-1

ACE85　Addressing the Spiritual Dimensions of Adult Learning: What Educators Can Do
Leona M. English, Marie A. Gillen
The contributors discuss how mentoring, self-directed learning, and dialogue can be used to promote spiritual development, and advocate the learning covenant as a way of formalizing the sanctity of the bond between learners and educators. Drawing on examples from continuing professional education, community development, and health education, they show how a spiritual dimension has been integrated into adult education programs.
ISBN 0-7879-5364-4

ACE84　An Update on Adult DFevelopment Theory: New Ways of Thinking About the Life Course
M. Carolyn Clark, Rosemary J. Caffarella
This volume presents discussions of well-established theories and new perspectives on learning in adulthood. Knowles' andragogy, self-directed learning, Mezirow's perspective transformation, and several other models are assessed for their contribution to our understanding of adult learning. In addition, recent theoretical orientations, including consciousness and learning, situated cognition, critical theory, and feminist pedagogy, are discussed in terms of how each expands the knowledge base of adult learning.
ISBN 0-7879-1171-2

ACE83　The Welfare-to-Work Challenge for Adult Literacy Educators
Larry G. Martin, James C. Fisher
Welfare reform and workforce development legislation has had a dramatic impact on the funding, implementation, and evaluation of adult basic education and literacy programs. This issue provides a framework for literacy practitioners to better align their field with the demands of the Work First environment and to meet the pragmatic expectations of an extended list of stakeholders.
ISBN 0-7879-1170-4

ACE82　Providing Culturally Relevant Adult Education: A Challenge for the Twenty-First Century
Talmadge C. Guy
This issue offers more inclusive theories that focus on how learners construct meaning in a social and cultural context. Chapters identify ways

that adult educators can work more effectively with racially, ethnically, and linguistically marginalized learners, and explore how adult education can be an effective tool for empowering learners to take control of their circumstances.
ISBN 0-7879-1167-4

ACE79   **The Power and Potential of Collaborative Learning Partnerships**
Iris M. Saltiel, Angela Sgroi, Ralph G. Brockett
This volume draws on examples of collaborative partnerships to explore the many ways collaboration can generate learning and knowledge. The contributors identify the factors that make for strong collaborative relationships, and they reveal how these partnerships actually help learners generate knowledge and insights well beyond what each brings to the learning situation.
ISBN 0-7879-9815-X

ACE77   **Using Learning to Meet the Challenges of Older Adulthood**
James C. Fisher, Mary Alice Wolf
Combining theory and research in educational gerontology with the practice of older adult learning and education, this volume explores issues related to older adult education in academic and community settings. It is designed for educators and others concerned with the phenomenon of aging in America and with the continuing development of the field of educational gerontology.
ISBN 0-7879-1164-X

ACE75   **Assessing Adult Learning in Diverse Settings: Current Issues and Approaches**
Amy D. Rose, Meredyth A. Leahy
Examines assessment approaches analytically from different programmatic levels and looks at the implications of these differing approaches. Chapters discuss the implications of cultural differences as well as ideas about knowledge and knowing and the implications these ideas can have for both the participant and the program.
ISBN 0-7879-9840-0

ACE70   **A Community-Based Approach to Literacy Programs: Taking Learners' Lives into Account**
Peggy A. Sissel
Encouraging a community-based approach that takes account of the reality of learners' lives; this volume offers suggestions for incorporating knowledge about a learner's particular context, culture, and community into adult literacy programming.
ISBN 0-7879-9867-2

ACE69   **What Really Matters in Adult Education Program Planning: Lessons in Negotiating Power and Interests**
Ronald M. Cervero, Arthur L. Wilson
Identifies issues faced by program planners in practice settings and the actual negotiation strategies they use. Argues that planning is generally conducted within a set of personal, organizational, and social relationships among people who may have similar, different, or conflicting interests, and that the program planner's responsibility centers on how to negotiate these interests to construct an effective program.
ISBN 0-7879-9866-4

**NEW DIRECTIONS FOR
ADULT AND CONTINUING EDUCATION
IS NOW AVAILABLE ONLINE AT WILEY INTERSCIENCE**

What is Wiley InterScience?

Wiley InterScience is the dynamic online content service from John Wiley & Sons delivering the full text of over 300 leading scientific, technical, medical, and professional journals, plus major reference works, the acclaimed *Current Protocols* laboratory manuals, and even the full text of select Wiley print books online.

What are some special features of Wiley InterScience?

Wiley InterScience Alerts is a service that delivers table of contents via e-mail for any journal available on Wiley InterScience as soon as a new issue is published online.
Early View is Wiley's exclusive service presenting individual articles online as soon as they are ready, even before the release of the compiled print issue. These articles are complete, peer-reviewed, and citable.
CrossRef is the innovative multi-publisher reference linking system enabling readers to move seamlessly from a reference in a journal article to the cited publication, typically located on a different server and published by a different publisher.

How can I access Wiley InterScience?

Visit http://www.interscience.wiley.com

Guest Users can browse Wiley InterScience for unrestricted access to journal Tables of Contents and Article Abstracts, or use the powerful search engine.
Registered Users are provided with a *Personal Home Page* to store and manage customized alerts, searches, and links to favorite journals and articles. Additionally, Registered Users can view free Online Sample Issues and preview selected material from major reference works.
Licensed Customers are entitled to access full-text journal articles in PDF, with select journals also offering full-text HTML.

How do I become an Authorized User?

Authorized Users are individuals authorized by a paying Customer to have access to the journals in Wiley InterScience. For example, a university that subscribes to Wiley journals is considered to be the Customer. Faculty, staff and students authorized by the university to have access to those journals in Wiley InterScience are Authorized Users. Users should contact their Library for information on which Wiley journals they have access to in Wiley InterScience.

ASK YOUR INSTITUTION ABOUT WILEY INTERSCIENCE TODAY!